The Villages of Aberdeen
Round About Mounthooly

In the late eighteenth century, Mounthooly experienced momentous changes; the great surge northwards of the city after Culloden; the arrival of the Aberdeenshire Canal and the Inverurie turnpike at its very heart; the industrial growth of the area which continued from the early iron-founding days to the zenith of the great Aberdeen engineering firms.

'*Round About Mounthooly*,' says Diane Morgan 'was an enjoyable though frustrating book to write. Much that was part of Aberdeen's history happened there, yet much has vanished as though it had never been. It was a place of character and warm-heartedness. It would be a pity if those who lived and wrought around Mounthooly were forgotten.'

This, the second volume in the 'Villages' series, bears the usual hallmarks of Diane Morgan's writing: readability, a fresh approach to local history, careful scholarship, a feeling for the place, humour and a dash of controversy.

By the same author

'Villages of Aberdeen' series

Footdee
and her Shipyards

Front Cover
The Mounthooly Newsagent and the Mount Pleasant Arch
From the original watercolour by J. A. Sutherland

The Villages of Aberdeen

Round About Mounthooly

Diane Morgan

Denburn Books
ABERDEEN

First Published 1995

© *Diane Morgan 1995*

All rights reserved. No part of this publication may
be reproduced in any form or by any means without
the prior permission of the publishers, Denburn Books,
49 Waverley Place Aberdeen AB1 1XP

British Library Cataloguing in Publication Data
A catalogue record for this book is available from the British Library

ISBN 1 898645 02 7

Design and Layout by
Jimmy and Pat Sutherland

Printed by Highland Printers Inverness

Acknowledgements

I am very grateful to the city archivist, Judith Cripps for her encouragement and advice, and to her staff for their assistance; to Alan R Fulton, Head of Library Services, and the staff of the Local Collection at Aberdeen City Libraries, superlative as always; to the Grampian Regional Archivist, Brenda Cluer, with a special word of thanks to her assistant, Patricia Douglas, who has nobly held the fort; to everyone at the Special Collections at King's College, University of Aberdeen; to Frank Donnelly for his sterling help with photography.

My thanks go to the following for sharing their memories which have greatly enriched the book: Alan Anderson, Anne Brand (Mrs Logan), Isobel and Tommy Donaldson, George Gordon, the Reverend Laurie Gordon, Joan Gray (Mrs MacMillan), Norah Morrison (Mrs Fairless), David Ross, Alex and Muriel Slessor, Mrs Walker (nee Fyfe) - whom we met by chance outside the Mounthooly Newsagent - and Jimmy Yule; with a special word of thanks to a former head of Causewayend School, Flora Youngson, and to the present head, Alistair P Mackay.

I am much indebted to those who have so readily given me the benefit of their technical expertise: Mike Dey of Aberdeen Art Gallery & Museums, Barry Craigmile of W McKinnon & Co, Ernest Muller of Mulco Engineers, Dr John S Reid and John A Souter. My thanks to R J Williamson, former editor of the *Evening Express* for his assistance, to Keith Jones and Jimmy Brown for being railway detectives and to G A Brown and Frank Reilly at AMEC for their interest.

I owe much to my book designers, Pat and Jimmy Sutherland, who have worked so hard and so ably to prepare this volume for publication; and to my husband, David I Morgan, who has patiently chauffeured me round about Mounthooly on countless occasions. There are less taxing things to do on a Sunday afternoon than to drive round this one-way-traffic-system (to give the roundabout its Sunday name), attempting to work out exactly where everything that is gone once was.

I am grateful to everyone who provided illustrations outwith the author's collection, and have acknowledged them individually. The front cover and the line drawings are by Jimmy (J A) Sutherland.

Diane Morgan, 1995

Contents

The view from the Gallowgate-head looking south to Windy Wynd, right. Or as we now say, the view from the Mounthooly roundabout to Spring Garden. Here an attractive range of student accommodation has replaced the Spring Garden Iron Works of W McKinnon & Co. The Gallowgate's multi-storey flats left, and the high rise building of the Aberdeen College right, tower behind.

Introduction

The best-laid schemes o mice an men
Gang aft agley
To a Mouse. Robert Burns

I have an apology to make to readers.

After finishing *Footdee*, the first volume in the 'Villages' series, I decided the next on the list should be *Old Aberdeen*. I would start at Mounthooly, a paragraph or two would suffice, while the Spital might even merit a chapter to itself. All this would be by way of introduction, before getting down to the main subject of the work.

It soon became evident that the Spital would require a book of its own. It was neither fish nor fowl, belonging neither to Aberdeen nor Old Aberdeen, those towns only laying claim to it when some advantage was to be had. It was an entity in itself. Very well then, *The Spital* as a separate volume in the 'Village' series would precede *Old Aberdeen*. There would be a chapter on Mounthooly by way of introduction... I need say no more.

Writing about Mounthooly has been a unique and fascinating voyage of discovery. The story begins at the Gallowgate-head, the ancient cross-roads where the major roads of the day met; the Gallowgate, heading south into Aberdeen, the Buchan and Inverurie highways going north and north west, the Old Skene Road going west and even the Back Causeway which later became West North Street going east. Our tale also ends at the Gallowgate-head - better known today as the Mounthooly roundabout - which contains a public park within its mighty circumference.

In the late eighteenth century, Mounthooly found itself at the heart of momentous changes; the great surge northwards of the city after Culloden; the coming of the Aberdeenshire Canal and the Inverurie turnpike into its very heart; the industrial growth of the area which continued from the early ironfounding days to the zenith of the great Aberdeen engineering

1

firms whose names were renowned worldwide.

But *Round About Mounthooly* does not merely charter growth and development. This is above all the story of a community - of several in fact - the close knit, and friendly communities of Mounthooly, Causewayend and Porthill, indeed of all who lived around the Gallowgate-head. The way of life, the kirks, the schools, the personalities, and these superlative community centres, the local shoppies, are recalled, as is their passing. Mounthooly has suffered more devastation than most communites, and even more after the war - though of the bloodless variety - than during it. That latter day upheaval was carried out in a good cause; rehousing, redevelopment and road improvement. And so, for twenty years now, the high rise flats and the articulated lorry have reigned supreme.

Should the roundabout have been built on such a massive scale? As one looks towards the city from Causewayend or Mounthooly, one can argue that it forms part of a wide and impressive vista, though marred at least for me, by the multi-storey 'courts', Seaton and Porthill, Hutcheon and Greig. High rise flats can look spectacular in an appropriate setting, but these dominate the townscape and they are nae bonnie. Perhaps when they reach the end of their natural life, they will be replaced by more sympathetic buildings.

On the bright side, restorations of fine, substantial tenements, and the building of new residential accommodation to a human scale in Nelson Street, Gerrard Street, Spring Garden and elsewhere has been carried out mainly, though not exclusively by the City of Aberdeen. Can this point the way to a new, more satisfactory environment round about Mounthooly?

Round About Mounthooly has been an enjoyable though frustrating book to write. So much happened here and now so much of the area has vanished as though it had never been. Before the massive changes of the 1960s and 1970s it was a place of great character and warm-heartedness and it would indeed be a pity if those who lived and wrought around Mounthooly were forgotten. It is to their memory that this book is dedicated.

On a technical note, I have followed the modern spelling of Gerrard Street, though, Gilbert Gerard and his father Alexander might not approve, but have stuck to John Maberly's spelling of his street. *The Spital* and *Old Aberdeen* have now been taken off the back burner, and my thanks to everyone who has been in touch about these projects. In addition, the siren voice of *Kittybrewster* is calling.

Part One

The Coming of the Turnpike

Nos 1 - 3 Mounthooly

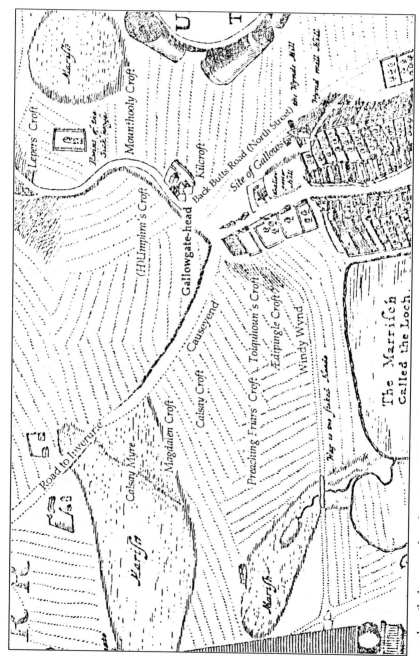

Lepers' Croft

Marsh

Bones & the lick holed spot

Mounthooly Croft.

Kilcroft

Back Butts Road (North Street)

(H)Umphin's Croft

Gallowgate-head

Site of Gallows

Causeyend

Calsay Croft

Calsay Myre

Magdalen Croft

Road to Inverurie

Preaching Friars' Croft

Toiquhoun's Croft

Fairpingle Croft

Windy Wynd

Marsh

Marsh

The Marish called the Loch.

'... where the houses and yards peter out.' The Gallowgate-head in 1661. A detail from Parson Gordon's Plan with the possible sites of the crofts superimposed.

4

Chapter 1

Around the Gallowgate-head

The Gallowgate-head...for convenience and situation, seldom to be met with.
Aberdeen Journal, January 27, 1808

Our journey begins at the Gallowgate-head. Today it lies buried below
the vast Mounthooly roundabout, but it was, and in its modern metamor-
phosis remains one of the most important crossroads in Aberdeen. It
appears in Parson Gordon's Plan of 1661, a bare-looking place where the
houses and yards of the town peter out. Five roads met there, three of them
major routeways in their day. Firstly the Gallowgate itself, the ancient road
north out of town. As its name indicates, it was the *gate* (Scots: a road) to the
gallows, and deserves a book to itself. Just to confuse matters, *port*, from the
French, is a gate, and the Gallowgate Port, one of the six city gates that
preserved Aberdonians from the hostile and the pestilent, stood near the
east end of Spring Garden where the student accommodation is now to be
found. Long before Gordon's time these ports were regarded as ancient but
it was not until 1769 that the Town Council decreed that the Gallowgate Port
and two others be 'immediately taken down and removed'. Traffic had
increased and there were numerous complaints that they were causing
obstructions. *Plus ça change, plus c'est la même chose.*

The Gallowgate Port gave its name to the Porthill which in Parson
Gordon's day was the highest of Aberdeen's hills. It is still with us, though
not as steep as it once was, starting a gentle rise at the 'new' Berry Street. The
gallows themselves were sited just outside the Port on the east side, while

Descending the Porthill towards the Gallowgate-head, from an old print.

the Porthill 'Wynde Mill' built in 1602 by order of the Town Council, was nearby, perhaps replacing an earlier one on the same site. Unlike the gallows which had been relocated near where Pittodrie Stadium now stands, the windmill seems to have been still in use in Gordon's time. He noted that the Porthill or Gallowgate-hill was 'ordinerlie callit the Windmill Hill, because of the wind milne situated upon the tope theroff'. Just outside the Port there stood the Porthill Factory, later known as 'the old Barracks' five-storeys high and dating from 1750. In *Aberdeen of Old*, (1986) Edward Meldrum described it as a building of coursed granite masonry, very large for its date:

> It comprised a four-sided courtyard entered from Seamount Place through a gateway with a bell bracket above. The entrance door of the east range was reached by a fine double flight curved staircase of classical design...This unique and interesting industrial building was demolished in 1960, after which its site was built over by residential development.

The modern marker for the Porthill's descent towards the Gallowgate-head is part of that residential development, the multi-storey Porthill Court, dating with its neighbour, Seamount Court, from the early 1960s. The Porthill's eastern foothills, once formidable, now make only a token

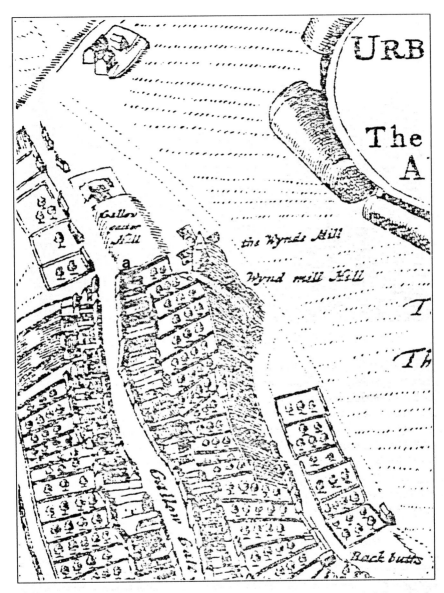

This detail from Gordon's Plan of 1661 shows the Windmill, and to its left, 'a' marks the site of the Gallowgate Port. 'Gallowgaites Hill' is the Porthill, a little community separate from the Gallowgate. At the top is the anonymous enclosure with three biggings which could indicate an early settlement at Mounthooly, while running from 'Wynd mill Hill' to the 'Back Butts' and beyond is the future West North Street. Compare the same view, from the east, by Gregory Sharpe on page 11.

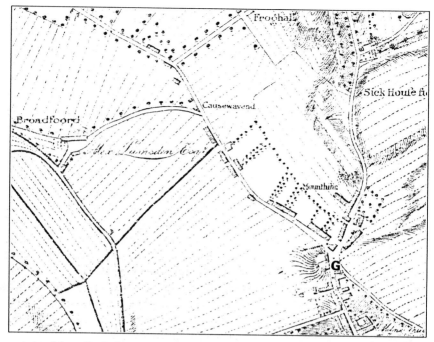

A detail from Taylor's Plan of 1773 showing the Gallowgate-head (G), and the settlements of 'Mounthilie' and of Causewayend, whose cottages flank the ancient highway to Inverurie near the junction with the 'litill cassy', the present Powis Lane. The Broadford shown was north of the one we know today.

descent to West North Street. Set a little apart from the rest of the Gallowgate, Porthill formed a community of its own which continued long after the Port was declared redundant.

Two other major tracks at the Gallowgate-head are shown on Gordon's Plan, both northerly and forming a fork. The right-hand track ran to Ellon and the Buchan hinterland via Mounthooly, the Spital, Old Aberdeen and the Brig o' Balgownie. It was one of the most important - and one of the worst - highways in the country.

No settlement at Mounthooly is noted by Gordon, though a substantial but anonymous enclosure with three biggings, south of the 'Ruins of the Sick house', may indicate a farm toon there. By 1746 however, 'Mount Hody' has appeared on G & W Paterson's Survey of Old and New Aberdeen, running north-east at the Gallowgate-head, with a handful of cottages tenaciously straddling the road, while the later Plans of both Taylor (1773) and Milne (1789) show 'Mount Hilie' as a sizeable and fairly compact clachan. Although Mounthooly lay at the start of the highway north, it was isolated from the Spital and Old Aberdeen. The low-lying, wild and

8

dangerous Howe o' Spital, flanked by the hilly Spital Lands to the west and marshes to the east had to be negotiated first. Mounthooly people would have considered the folk of the Porthill, and the crofters of Causewayend as their neighbours rather than those of the Spital and Old Aberdeen.

Returning to Gordon's Plan, the other major road, the left-hand fork running north-west from the Gallowgate-head, was the ancient highway to Inverurie. While still within the Inner Marches it passed the northern crofts of the town then, and took to high ground, as was customary with ancient highways confronted by marshland, at what became Canal Road, crossing to the Outer Marches near where the Froghall Railway bridge is now sited. At the future Elmbank Terrace it was met by a north-easterly track which led off to Wester Peter, later Froghall, and a little further along, by another path that led to Sunnyside Farm, and subsequently also gave access to Sunnybank House. Here the air was still and sweet with the scent of wildflowers, though by the 1850s the calm of this pleasant country walk would be interrupted by the distant hooting of engines at Kittybrewster and the noise of wagons rattling along the Kittybrewster-Waterloo line below. This section of the old Inverurie highway formed the boundary between the Spital Lands to the north and the Lands of Calsayseat, owned since 1705 by the Frasers of Powis to the west. Causewayend was a part of these lands, but it was not quite the Causewayend we know today.

The old highway now runs out of our story, past the substantial farm toon of Berryhillock, its fields stretching westwards to Berryden. Berryhillock was also part of the Lands of Calsayseat and today would sit near Powis Terrace, at Split-the-Wind. After passing the clachan of Peterstown and 'Ketty Brewster's Howe' the highway climbed the future Clifton Road which was at the heart of the Lands of Peterstown, then on to Persley, Bankhead, Greenburn, and so to Inverurie. Greenburn is now recalled only by Greenburn Road, but for a period after 1701 when an Act of Parliament authorised its laird, James Moir of Stoneywood, to hold two yearly fairs, Hagg Fair in June and Bathie Fair in July, it enjoyed a period of prominence. So important was Greenburn in its heyday that the old highway was sometimes described as 'the High Road leading to Greenburn' rather than 'to Inverury'.

Gordon's Plan also shows two 'B roads' as we might loosely call them, converging at the Gallowgate-head, which can be mentioned in passing. One of these ran behind the gallows and the Porthill windmill, hugged the east side of the long Gallowgate gardens, and passed through a rural enclave, the Back Butts, before reaching the north side of the Castlegate. By the eighteenth century this track had been upgraded to become North Street, and to provide an important link between the Gallowgate-head and points north, and Virginia Street, Commerce Street and the Quay. Bisected by King Street at the beginning of the nineteenth century, the eastern part of this road became East North Street, while its westerly counterpart continued as North Street. By the 1830s however, 'West' was being prefixed in various documents and twenty years later West North Street had become official.

The second 'B road,' was the 'Way to the Stocked Heade', which struck out due west near the Gallowgate-head from its starting point at Windy Wynd as it does to this day. It took the traveller to Alford on the Old Skene Road via what is now Maberly Street, Rosemount Place, Midstocket Road and the Lang Stracht. Windy Wynd ran as far as the junction with Lochside, later Loch Street, at which point its line was continued westwards along the Spring Gardens which lay south of the Broadford Meadows, implying a climatic variation from storm to sunshine in quite a small area. The spring in question could have been the watery rather than the seasonal variety. The town's early mills were powered by a series of lades, one of which flowed here on its way south to the Loch-Eye, a dam which was all that remained of the ancient Loch of Aberdeen. 'Gardens' may have been a reference to the willows which had been planted alongside the lade.

The landscape surrounding the two northerly highways as they left the Gallowgate-head would have been less bleak than it looks on Gordon's Plan. In their initial stages within the Inner Marches the highways were flanked by the northern crofts of the burgh, noted in title deeds from the fifteenth century onwards and whose feudal superiors included leading local families, the Church, and following the Reformation, the University of King's College and Marischal College. This was not the sort of crofting we know today, but the cultivation of strips of land, sometimes little more than 'plotties' by the cumbersome runrig method in which neighbouring strips would be tended by different tenants. Bere, an early form of barley, was grown, along with oats and perhaps rye, a little wheat and 'pease'. After harvest, cattle from the byres of Broad Street and the Gallowgate would be herded along to forage amidst the stubble and to fertilise the soil. Clumsy and inefficient though the runrig system was, it provided the burgh with the raw materials to produce ale and bannocks at a time when the transport of cereals, or anything else for that matter, over any distance, was difficult.

These crofts cannot be pinpointed with accuracy but an attempt has been made on page 14 to plot a few around the Gallowgate-head, based on descriptions in feu charters and other documents. Going from east to west were Thorniebalk Croft which may have been part of the settlement of Mounthooly and the Lepers' Croft a little to the north where King's Crescent Fire Station is now sited. At the Gallowgate-head itself was the

The mass of the Porthill, right, hides part of the Galowgate in this detail from Gregory Sharpe's East Prospect of Aberdeen, 1732. 'b' indicates Provost Fordyce's summer house, and 'c', the Porthill Windmill, in ruins by this time. The Spital Road to Old Aberdeen leads off, extreme right. 'Y', centre, is part of the Gallowgate, 'V', left, is the rear of Marischal College with its garden below. The small plot of land immediately right is the Back Butts which at this time had a bowling green. The path hugging the foot of the Porthill, Back Butts and College Garden was the future West North Street.

Kilcroft 'with Kyll barne, yard and taill (garden) adjacent'. *Kil* or *kyll* is a kiln and the 'Kyll barne' might have been worked in conjunction with the nearby Porthill windmill. Crofts sometimes changed names as they changed ownership, but in the fork between Mounthooly and the Inverurie Highway, Umphraye's or Humphrey's Croft long retained that name, albeit with a multiplicity of spellings, although William Umphra himself had died before 1540.

Moving west, Tolquhoun's Croft seems to have been larger than most and had once belonged to the Preaching Friars. It was granted by King James VI to the Earl Marischal in 1592 and so came into the possession of Marischal College. The neighbouring Ædipingle Croft passed to King's College after the Reformation. It was the practice in those days to name each member of the university as well as his chair in fueing transactions, which makes interesting reading. In 1758, for example, a feu charter relating to a part of Ædipingle Croft in favour of an Aberdeen farmer, Robert Duncan, was granted by all ten members of King's College, including Dr John Gregory, Professor of Medicine, one of the famous scientific and medical Gregories, and Mr Thomas Reid, Professor of Philosophy and one of the greatest thinkers of his age or any other.

Further west, the Croft of the Altar of St Mary Magdalene and its neighbour, 'a croft callit ye Calsay Croft', and the Cruikit Myre were later incorporated into the Lands of Broadford which George Fordyce, thrice provost between 1718 and 1727, acquired, and where there had indeed been a broad ford. The traveller and writer, Francis Douglas, with his sharp eye for agricultural improvements, thought highly of the Provost's labours. In his *General Description of the East Coast* (1782), Douglas noted that the low swampy ground around Broadford:

> has been accurately drained and intersected with sunk stone fences; it is a perfect model of draining, and has liberally repaid the expence laid out upon it.

Hugh Hutcheon, advocate and speculator, was a later laird of Broadford and son-in-law of Alexander Leslie, proprietor of the fantastic pleasance of neighbouring Berryden.

Change was the order of the day as the Agricultural Revolution gained in impetus during the eighteenth century. 'Improving' lairds and farmers in the North-east were anxious to replace the muddy and often impassable local roads (for 'highway' read muddy track) with the well-constructed new roads, financed by tolls, which were progressing gradually further north. These took their name from the turnpike or spiked barrier at the toll-gate, and though still built by pick and shovel were surveyed and engineered by men of the calibre of Macadam, Rennie and Telford. A network of turnpike roads in Aberdeenshire would facilitate the transport of fertilisers required for the more advanced new crops, and would allow farmers to become more adventurous in marketing them. Moreover, those lairds, farmers and merchants who invested in the new roads hoped,(often in vain), for a quick return. In 1795, an Act of Parliament was passed to provide turnpike roads for the County of Aberdeen and a mammoth road construction programme quickly got underway. One aspect of the improvement in communications would be reflected by the number of markets in Aberdeenshire which had risen to 180 by 1811 compared with around fifty a century earlier.

The story of the 'home' stages of the Inverurie Turnpike which superseded the old 'Highway to Inverury' is an interesting one. Mooted in 1798, the route was mapped out by Charles Abercrombie, a well known Edinburgh surveyor. After passing through Woodside and Kittybrewster it was to enter Aberdeen via the Gallowgate-head as before, though the old highway's path over hilly ground at the future Elmbank Terrace-Canal Road area would be replaced by a realigned route, the straight, flat Powis

Place-Causewayend road we know today. But both Abercrombie and the turnpike trustees had failed to take into consideration the fact that the city's growth northwards was in a line west of the proposed turnpike route.

This expansion had started after Culloden, a matter of necessity, for the population had almost trebled from 5,556 souls in 1708 to 15,730 by 1755. In 1754 the Town Council took action, opening a new street which they eventually 'ordained to be callit Tannerie' from the Schoolhill-Upperkirkgate junction to the south end of the dam at the Loch-Eye. North of Tannery Street lay the Lochlands, lands long ago reclaimed from the Loch and owned by James Staats Forbes, an entrepreneurial Queen Street china merchant. In 1783 they were parcelled into lots and sold. The Lochland streets would include St Andrew Street, Charlotte Street and John Street, at right angles to the principal street, George Street which would continue in a line from Tannery Street, opening up the town to the north, towards the Spring Gardens and Broadford.

Now with three colleagues, including Hugh Hutcheon, proprietor of Broadford, James Staats Forbes suggested to the turnpike trustees that the Inverurie Turnpike should enter Aberdeen by a new road which would link Kittybrewster with the newly laid out George Street, at that time just a short and narrow street, and Tannery Street. This 'direct, level and elegant access to the Town', the foursome maintained, was much preferable to the 'narrow, and steep access by the Gallowgate'. However the consortium's proposed total investment of £850 gave them a fair measure of 'clout' and they offered additional inducements.

One might guess that they were not entirely motivated by concern for elegance in town planning, for the group stood to do well financially if the turnpike came through their land. On the other hand, if the original Causewayend plan went ahead, development might be stimulated there to the detriment of George Street. It was no doubt a considerable relief to the Staats Forbes consortium when the turnpike trustees approved the 'George's Street' route in 1799.

A member of the turnpike committee now started to cause trouble. One could not be blamed for assuming that this was Hugh Leslie, laird of Powis, who would stand to lose if the turnpike were diverted from Causewayend which formed part of the Lands of Calsayseat which he owned. But Leslie had invested only £50 in the turnpike and seems to have been more interested in the arts, agriculture and arguments with his colleagues at King's College than in speculation. No, the fly in the ointment was the awkward and quarrelsome Alexander Shand of Tanfield in Woodside who began to argue that the trustees had no right to alter the route. Subscriptions, he maintained, had originally been raised on the

13

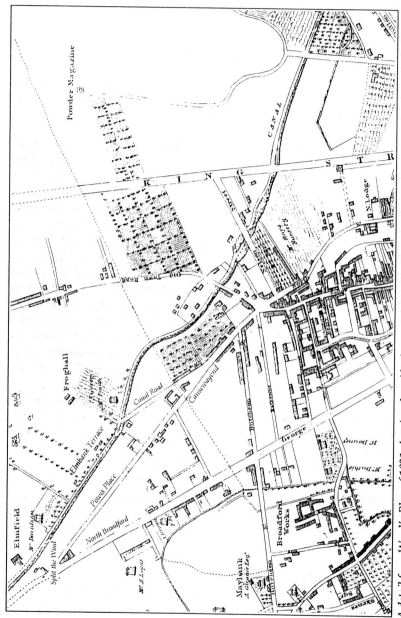

A detail from Wood's Plan of 1821 showing the widening out of the Aberdeenshire Canal at Nelson Street. Roy's Nursery is south of Nelson Street.

14

understanding that the Causewayend-Gallowgate route would be followed. The Staats Forbes' plan went ahead, however. After Kittybrewster, the turnpike passed through the Lands of Broadford and at the Spring Gardens it met George Street which was extended in width to match it. But Shand continued to make trouble of one sort or another and the trustees conceded that he had a point. They agreed that the Causewayend-Gallowgate route should be laid out as originally envisaged. The turnpike would split just south of Kittybrewster, at North Broadford, and the junction thus created was soon nicknamed Split-the-Wind.

The George Street approach, under the eagle eye of the Staats Forbes consortium was up and running very quickly. The Causewayend route, however, found that it had another rival shadowing it in the shape of the Aberdeen-Inverurie or Aberdeenshire Canal. 'Shape' is perhaps not the best word. The final section of the canal, from Kittybrewster to Waterloo Quay, was being surveyed at this time, and there was some doubt as to where exactly it would go. But turnpike and canal would run in close proximity on the Kittybrewster-Gallowgate-head stretch, and work on the turnpike could not go ahead until the fine tuning on the waterway was complete. At last, the ultimate stage of the canal route was finalised. From Kittybrewster it would hug the old highway, flowing alongside the future Elmbank Terrace as far as Froghall where the road would be carried over the canal by a bridge. It would then head a little to the north, but parallel to Canal Road and Causewayend before striking out cross country and passing under bridges at Mounthooly, Nelson Street and King Street. Eventually it would curve due south at Constitution Street and make its leisurely way to the Links and to Waterloo Quay. Its course is shown on the map opposite and it can easily be followed today, for the Kittybrewster-Harbour railway line was laid out directly on the canal bed. Stand today at the King Street bridge, looking up to Nelson Street and it is possible to imagine the canal flowing turgidly downstream.

The Causewayend section of the turnpike now went ahead and was completed in 1802. The tempo of life at the Gallowgate-head must have quickened considerably when the Inverurie Turnpike to the west, the North or Ellon Turnpike to the east and the Aberdeenshire Canal flowing through the centre appeared, all of them more or less simultaneously.

Three new streets, Gerrard, Catherine and Hutcheon, running north of Windy Wynd and parallel to it, linked the west side of the Gallowgate-head with the Inverurie Turnpike. Nelson Street on the east side made the link with King Street, the home stretch of the Ellon Turnpike. Nelson Street had been feued out in December 1805, two months after the Battle of Trafalgar,

15

and since the Shipmaster Society of Aberdeen owned land there, it was likely they who named it in honour of their heroic colleague. Though King Street itself was a more satisfactory and straightforward route than the obstacle course that constituted the north highway via Old Aberdeen, it was, nevertheless, slow to feu out and for many years was not built up much beyond Mealmarket Street. Yet further north, Nelson Street enjoyed a dynamism that was created by the Aberdeenshire Canal. The canal had been widened on both sides of the Nelson Street bridge so that barges could pass each other, and there was a wet dock between Nelson Street and Mounthooly where they could be pulled to the side and overhauled. An access road from the Gallowgate-head led to the canal, crossing what later became John Knox's Kirkyard. Here barrows filled with a few tools and whatever materials were necessary for repairs would be wheeled down to the canal bank and the clang of hammers and the shouts of bargees would resound round Nelson Street and the Gallowgate-head.

By the early nineteenth century ten streets radiated from the Gallowgate-head. Windy Wynd, which we can include at a pinch, Gerrard, Catherine and Hutcheon Streets to the west, Causewayend and the Spital to the north, the canal access road and Nelson Street to the west, then North Street and the Gallowgate itself where we began.

Chapter 2

Causewayend and Calsayseat

Cassie, cassy, calsay, causey: Scots forms of English *causeway*. A cobbled street or pavement.

Scottish National Dictionary

The Causewayend we know today is a street which runs from Mounthooly to Powis Place, but the word originally indicated the place where the 'causeway' or the cassies of the town came to an end. Aberdeen's original Causewayend was just such a place, a settlement at the edge of the town, north-west of the Gallowgate-head, in today's terms, around the top of Canal Road, Elmbank Terrace and the surrounding land. Cassie or Causey-end as it was often called, lay within the Lands of Calsayseat, once part of the Royal Forest of Stocket. In 1562 James Leslie was granted by the burgh and magistrates :

a pece west ground lyand within the freedom of Abirdene upon the north syd of the litill cassy merchand with the Spitell heritable in feu to big ane barne and barn yard.

Here, in what became the Lands of Calsayseat, Leslie could have built numerous barns, for it seems that he had acquired ground stretching north almost as far as Kittybrewster, marching with Elmbank Terrace to the east and what is now Berryden Road to the west. The southern boundary, whose central point was the 'litill cassy' - Powis Lane - was just beyond the Inner Marches of the burgh.

The piece of waste ground granted to Leslie did not imply a rubbish dump. It could be marshland, or an area of gorse and whins, with the potential to be cleared and cultivated. However Leslie and his successors were expressly forbidden from cultivating the 'gettis' or gates that ran through their land, including the stretch of the highway to Inverurie which, having left the Gallowgate-head and skirted Tolqhhoun's croft, took the high ground at what would become Canal Road and Elmbank Terrace, and so to Kittybrewster.

After Leslie's time, Calsayseat passed to other owners; notably to William Moir of Scotstown in 1602 and in 1713 to Alexander Fraser first laird of Powis and Professor of Greek at King's College, and subsequently to his descendants, another set of Leslies. We know the names of some of the Cassie-end farmers in Alexander Fraser's time. Norman Nicoll who farmed Berryhillock (around the Split-the-Wind-Powis Terrace area, spreading westwards), had a tack or lease from Fraser during the 1720s of 'part of the middle shade (strip) of the Lands of Cassie-end from the march balk (boundary ridge) of Alexander Leith's croft to the marish called Kettiebrouster'. Leith's croft, 'that Croft of Land with the houses, yeards and pertinents thereof lying in Cassie-end', had been worked by his family for three generations. Another farmer, Robert Murray, had tack of two crofts at Cassie-end by 1723, 'with the houses, biggings and yeards thereto belonging'. Rent was paid to Fraser both in cash and kind. Norman Nicoll's rent for example included thirteen bolls of bere, £4 10s Scots and 'ane dozen Powltrie Foulis'.

These charters provide a picture of farm toons and rigs, of cottages and enclosures, of hens scratching round the barnyards while the old maps show that the dwellings were scattered alongside the Inverurie highway. Cassie-end had its own blacksmith, masons, labourers, cowfeeder - the old name for a dairyman - shoemakers, gardeners, and a butcher: 'David Harrow, sometime flesher in Causey End who died December 7, 1780 aged 74 years' would have been a familiar figure. His gravestone, with its distinctive lettering can be seen in St Machar's Kirkyard. The Harrows continued their trade at Wales Street after the butcher market opened there in 1806.

By this time, however, the two home stretches of the new Inverurie turnpike had been laid out, parting company at North Broadford (George Street) just south of Kittybrewster to form the distinctive junction nicknamed Split-the-Wind. The Causewayend fork ran straight and true through the Lands of Calsayseat abandoning the future Elmbank Terrace-Canal Road stretch of the old Inverurie highway high and hopefully dry to the east, though both roads shared, as they still do, the last couple of

David Harrow's gravestone in St Machar's Kirkyard.

hundred yards to the Gallowgate-head.

Early nineteenth century title deeds attempted to make a clear distinction between the old highway to Inverurie and the new turnpike. In some, the old highway after it leaves the Gallowgate-head is described as 'the north side of Causewayend, formerly the High Road leading from Aberdeen to Greenburn' while the new road is 'the turnpike road leading from Aberdeen to Inverurie called Causewayend'. Confusion was caused by the fact that for some years Causewayend remained the blanket name for the whole area. Take, for example, Honeybank, the home of the merchant William Emslie, which sat in its own grounds overlooking the canal. Originally the address was Honeybank, Causewayend, then Honeybank, Canalside, followed by Honeybank, 'near Sutherland's manufactory', and finally plain No 52 Canal Road. Clarification came when 'Causewayend' became the specific name for the stretch of turnpike between the Gallowgatehead and Gowan Brae, the latter nowadays the north-east section of Fraser Place. It was rather nearer town than the original Lands of Cassie-end. By the 1830s, the place where the old highway took to the high ground as it approached the old settlement of Causewayend, had established its separate identity as Canal Road, running 'from Causewayend to the Froghall Bridge'.

A view of Causewayend in 1974, showing right, one of the early tenement properties, demolished soon after. The building on the left remains and is now commercial premises. Courtesy, City of Aberdeen - Planning Division.

With the turnpike acting as an impetus, much of Causewayend around the junction with Mounthooly and as far along as the junction with Canal Road was under construction at this time. 'Tenements of dwelling houses and shops', as they are described in the old title deeds, some of them surviving until the 1970s, began to cover the old croftlands around the Gallowgate-head. Most were modest, of two storeys and attics, their chubby dormers springing out of the tiles. New properties frequently changed hands. The number of masons who appear as first owners, though for a very short period, indicate that some speculative building ventures were afoot. The future Nos 24-28 Causewayend is a good example. It was acquired in 1805 by a reedmaker, Robert Simmey from George Birnie, a Muggiemoss mason who had built a house there. In 1806 Simmey sold on to John Roy, merchant, who in 1807 sold on again, to James Knowles, Treasurer of the Narrow Wynd Society, Aberdeen's first Friendly Society. As landlords, they now retained the property for over half a century. For the city's friendly societies - there were about fifty at this time - the purchase of new properties for purposes of leasing was a useful form of income. In January 1808, for example, the following advertisement appeared in the *Aberdeen Journal:*

To let that house at the Gallowgate-head belonging to the Gordon's Mills Friendly Society consisting of Four Flats with Coomceiled Rooms (sloping ceilings) with Stables, large Hay Loft and Back Close shut in by itself. For convenience and situation seldom to be met with.

Over on the east side of the Gallowgate-head, Robert Connon, an Aberdeen cartwright, emerged briefly as the wheeler-dealer of that particular corner, but by 1810 had sold 'that piece of angular ground at the Gallowgate-head of Aberdeen', the future Mounthooly-West North Street junction, to another entrepreneur for £36 10s. The new owner was William Wildgoose, farmer at Sunnyside, and a tenant of Hugh Leslie of Powis. Houses were built there soon after.

The crop failure in Aberdeenshire in 1782 had brought country folk into town in search of work and there had also been a steady drift of Highlanders, recruited initially to work in local quarries. They formed a community of around 1000 by 1785. According to the *Bon-Accord Repository* of 1842, the population stood at over 35,370 by 1811, almost double the 1755 figure quoted in Chapter One. It rose again to 44,796 in 1821, the return of Napoleonic veterans in 1815 accounting for a small part of this increase. By 1841 it would be over 63,000. Although the Commutation Road Books for 1811-1812 reveal occupations in Causewayend that could be found in any country village, the arrival of industry in the area is indicated by a heckler who probably combed out the flax at the recently established Broadford Works nearby in Maberly Street, while a woolcomber, also noted, may have worked at the Causewayend Woollen Mill at one time run by Crombie & Co, whose manager, John Ramage, lived nearby at No 8 Catherine Street.

A few gentlemen in the Causewayend area had registered themselves as eligible to vote following the passage of the 1832 Reform Act, indicating that they owned or tenanted property valued at £10 or more per annum. These included the merchant William Emslie, John Elrick, a meal seller, James Laing a cabinet maker, and at No 56 Causewayend, Alexander Gildavie, Jnr, mason, whose father had been responsible for the bridge at Cults and harbour works at Footdee. The census returns of 1851, however, show a population that is substantially working class; flax spinners and flax dressers, yarn spinners, cotton spinners, handloom weavers and comb and horn spoon makers who would have been employed at the mighty Comb Works along in Hutcheon Street. Later census returns show a widening of occupations; bookbinders, slaters, carpenters, paperworkers, a paraffin refiner, a gatekeeper. They also reveal that about fifty percent of Causewayend folk hailed from outwith the 'home' parishes of St Nicholas and Old Machar. They came from Belhelvie, Foveran, Peterhead, Old Deer,

Coull, Keith, Gamrie, Fettercairn and Kintore, to name but a few areas. David Mitchell, for example, a policemen living in Causewayend came from Logie Buchan, his wife from Tarves.

If a sequence of poor harvests and the replacement of the old run rig system by more economic and efficient farming methods had originally driven redundant farm workers into the city, by the 1850s the new railways were also playing their part in this upheaval. Their arrival caused some country towns to boom, others, bypassed, to decline; those whose businesses failed as a result and those thrown out of work were likely to seek employment in Aberdeen where men with a rural background could quickly adapt to jobs on offer. Between them, the carting firms of Wordie & Co Ltd, established in Aberdeen in the 1850s, and Mutter Howey & Co Ltd, in the 1870s, both of whom were contractors for the railways, employed hundreds of carters of country stock over the years. The rural exodus of the late eighteenth century had continued into the nineteenth, during whose latter half there was a drift of 3,000 agricultural workers into Aberdeen. One can't help feeling that they all turned up in Causewayend!

Beyond Gowan Brae, the turnpike became the Causewayend Road, and as such carried on to Split-the-Wind. The Brae marked the end of the city's built-up area and the official boundary running across Causewayend between Hutcheon Street and Charles Street was close at hand. The Causewayend Road took one through virtually open country - though the area boasted the Glen Northton Distillery - past fields girt with high hawthorn hedges. Robert Anderson, 'an old Causewayend loon', leaves a memorable description of the area around the middle of the nineteenth century in *Aberdeen in Bygone Days* (1910):

In those days Powis Terrace and Powis Place were not; what is now the site of Causewayend United Free Church (St Stephen's) was the northern limit of the houses in Causewayend...Split-the-Wind then stood amid fields, mostly pasture ground or bleaching fields, a nursery on one hand, the entrance marked by the old-fashioned pair of whale jawbones, and on the other hand a bit of grazing land beloved of the children of the neighbourhood and known to them as 'the gowany park'. A few yards east ran the Aberdeenshire Canal, if its sluggish flow could be said to run.

Split-the-Wind shared its name with the inn there known locally as 'Splitties' or 'The Coffin' because it was so narrow. This busy junction was a popular meeting place for travellers, carters and carriers and anyone observing the turnpike from the future Elmbank Terrace would have enjoyed a colourful scene. Carriers' carts rumbling along on their last lap to town after a break for refreshment at 'The Coffin'; country folk in gigs;

The buildings at Split-the-Wind, looking towards the town. 'The Coffin' Inn is in the foreground, with Calsay Seat house behind. Powis Parish Church was built on this site in 1895. From the drawing by David Reid.

the four-in-hand stagecoaches rattling along, among them *Defiance*, the fastest stagecoach in Britain on the Edinburgh to Inverness run; the Inverurie-to-Aberdeen *Banks of Don* and the *Engineer* which did the same journey in reverse; the *Earl of Fife* on the Aberdeen to Banff run; the resplendent red and gold Royal Mail coaches with the lion and unicorn emblazoned on their panels and the drivers and guards in their lum hats and bright red coats.

George Street may have been the place for business and shopping, but the Causewayend approach was popular with coaches and carriers. On reaching the Gallowgate-head they could shun the precipitous Gallowgate in favour of the long stretch of North Street with its leisurely inclines and the inns and stables for which that area was well known. An advertisement in the *Aberdeen Journal* in September 1811 for the sale of a house and stable in North Street noted that 'the premises have long been used and well-frequented as a stabling'. The upset price of £600 was £60 more than that asked for Bailie Clarke's sizeable house and garden in Old Aberdeen in the same issue of the newspaper. North Street, moreover, gave access both to the Harbour and to the Links, which was handy when the Aberdeen Races were in progress there. William Smith, writing in the *Book of Powis* (1906), has an anecdote about 'a mischief of a horse', Little Jamie, and the hawthorn hedges of Causewayend. On one occasion while leading the field at the Links, Jamie broke away at the Gasworks corner, bolted along the neighbouring streets, careered along East and West North Streets, then Causewayend. He had almost reached Split-the-Wind when:

> running into a quick-set hedge, he stopped short. The jockey, however, went on straight through the stobs, and despite a scratching, thanked his stars when he landed in the field beyond for Jamie was just then in the humour to make a meal of his rider's leather breeches and what was inside them. After causing the death of three men and injuring others, this fiend of a horse was ultimately shot.

The Causewayend Road and the portion of the Lands of Calsayseat between Split-the-Wind and the future Berryden Road evolved very differently from the George Street Road. The Leslie lairds did not seem to have the same enthusiasm for urbanisation as Staats Forbes and his colleagues, and Hugh Leslie had been happy to enter into a treaty of excambion - a land swap - with Hugh Hutcheon of Broadford to accommodate the George Street Road. Far from taking advantage of the turnpike and feuing out their property for speculative development, they seemed more interested in encouraging the growth of small estates and of large houses set in landscaped grounds. In 1779 Hugh Leslie had given off land at Berryhillock to yet another Leslie, Alexander, a Broad Street druggist, who built Berryden House and laid out a pleasure garden in the grounds, including a fashionable hermitage. Hugh Leslie was much impressed and had a hermitage built for himself at Powis. With a family of fourteen he perhaps felt the need of a personal retreat.

This certainly was prior to the coming of the turnpike, but even after its arrival the Leslies continued their 'country house' policy. Some time before 1821 when John Leslie, Hugh's son was laird, the House of Calsay Seat was built at Split-the-Wind, at the site of Berryhillock farmhouse, 'with the gables facing to George Street and Causewayend'. It seems a curious place for gentry to choose for 'The Coffin' was next door. Another portion of Calsayseat, a little south-west of Split-the-Wind was given out in feu about the same time for the building of Millbank House whose history really belongs to George Street.

Hugh Fraser Leslie, a fiery-tempered but kind-hearted bachelor returned from Jamaica to take up his inheritance in 1848 after the death of his brother John. Their maternal grandfather, James Lamond, had been a Jamaica merchant and family property there, including a coffee plantation was inherited by their mother. She had dispatched Hugh, the second son, thither to administer it in 1823. He survived over twenty years on the disease-ridden island, but it was a sair trachle and he was no doubt glad to return to the Powis estates.

At first his accounts dealt mainly with wages and agricultural items including revenue from the sale of crops, and expenditure on manure and seeds. The area began to lose its rural charm, however, when the canal was replaced by the Great North of Scotland Railway. The line from Huntly to Kittybrewster opened in 1854 and the following year the tracks were laid along the canal bed from Kittybrewster to the Waterloo Quay ter-

Hugh Fraser Leslie of Powis.

minus. The canal bridges at Nelson Street and Mounthooly were supplanted by railway bridges allowing greater headroom while the Froghall bridge was replaced by another a hundred yards or so to the west, the Tarry Briggie, accounting in part for the curious layout at the Froghall-Canal Road junction which causes pedestrians to take their lives into their hands. The stagecoaches soon gave up the unequal struggle against the locomotive. The *Defiance* survived only a few weeks and 'The Coffin' became the Railway Tavern.

From the 1860s Hugh Fraser Leslie's records show his farming interests decreasing while details of ground being feued out for development at Causewayend and elsewhere become more frequent. In 1868 Leslie feued out two lots of land running north-west along the Causewayend Road from the Gowan Brae junction. This brought Hawthorn Place into being, taking its name from the hawthorn hedges that were a feature of the area. At the same time Leslie had given off feus at Split-the-Wind and a short row of houses, Powis Place, was built 'at Calsayseat'. Powis Place was very select, including among its first residents, two ministers and Mr Cardno of Cardno and Darling, seedsmen, whose renowned nurseries were nearby, at Kittybrewster.

The occupations of the residents in both Hawthorn and Powis Places - 'Place' had upmarket connotations - was an interesting mix, reflecting some superior housing. There were the usual weavers and combmakers, but also a shipmaster, a compositor, a chemical works overseer, cattle dealers, tea dealers, stonecutters, builders, a master blacksmith, a cooper and a joiner, a watchmaker, an electrician, an India rubber chainmaker(!) a teacher of classics, a student of theology, a civil servant, an insurance agent, a

Harry Gordon, Aberdeen's great comedian was undoubtedly Powis Place's most famous resident. He was born at No 7 on July 11, 1893, eldest of six children of David Gordon, a journeyman plumber and his wife. The family later moved to Urquhart Road.

commercial traveller, an umbrella maker, a flesher, a grain merchant, and William Low, mason diver, who was probably involved in repair work at the harbour. Hawthorn Place in its heyday was a favourite with dressmakers while Powis Place, so handy for Kittybrewster, was home to every conceivable category of railway worker from engine driver to 'blacksmith at railway works', a good example of a rural skill adapting to an urban environment. During the decade after its creation, Powis Place developed south-eastwards, annexed Hawthorn Place by 1880, and thus ran all the way 'from the north end of Causewayend to Calsayseat'. By now, the old name, the Causewayend Road, like the turnpike system itself, had vanished into oblivion. It may have seemed appropriate to keep the name 'Causewayend' right out to Split-the-Wind, but after passing the 'litill cassy' - Powis Lane - Powis Place acknowledged the start of Leslie land.

Truly an ill wind. The urbanisation of their territories gave the Leslies ample opportunity to indulge their mania for promoting the family names. While part of Powis Lane formed the base of the triangle that led to Split-the-Wind, Powis Place and its opposite number on the George Street side, Leslie Place, which also belonged to the Lands of Calsayseat, formed the arms. A row of urban cottages had been built there during the 1870s, and part of 'Calsayseat Cottage' can still be made out on the house nearest the former Split-the-Wind kirk.

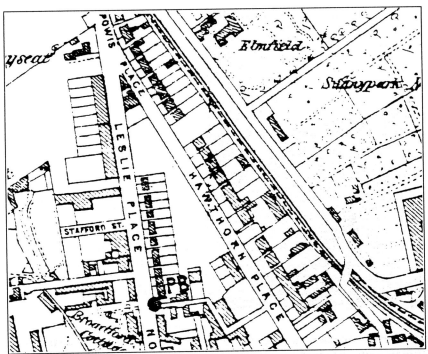

This Post Office Directory Plan of 1880 shows Leslie Place and Hawthorn Place linked by the Powis Lane dog-leg. Note the Split-the-Wind junction beside Powis Place.

The whole area teemed with life as the century drew to a close, with six or eight, sometimes nine families occupying the tall tenements and three, even four families in the cottages that sprinkled the area, some of them nestling in the little lanes that link Powis Place and George Street. In Powis Place itself, across on the north side there were a few 'back' houses overlooking the railway line, entered through closes. Best remembered among them are these lofty tenements, the 'Powis Barracks', home to numerous families. Before the area was completely built up, however, local children found it an admirable playground, though as the population increased, the hawthorn hedging deteriorated. The *Causewayend Free Church Bazaar Book* of 1900 noted that:

Its gnarled stems were often festooned with sundry bits of rope, clothes lines etc, made to do duty as swings, known as 'showdin tows'. Much capital fun resulted from the arrangement, frequent breaks and tumbles adding to the enjoyment. Sundry gaps in the old hedge, too, made it an ideal spot for 'tig' and other games...We doubt whether the amenities of the public parks have done better service to young Aberdeen than did this old bit of greenery ere it was given over to the pick and shovel and replaced by hard-hearted granite walls.

The Misses Leslie, the sisters of Hugh Fraser Leslie lived at Calsay Seat for a time, while the laird himself maintained a bachelor establishment at Powis House. Although they were amply compensated, things were never quite the same for the family after the erosion of their estates by the railway complex at Kittybrewster and the building of the Denburn Valley Railway between Kittybrewster and the new Joint Station during 1865-67, part of which ran through Calsayseat. After Hugh's death in 1873, his five surviving sisters, moved to Powis House and Calsay Seat was tenanted for nearly twenty years by the family of James Souttar, architect of the Imperial Hotel and the Salvation Army Citadel. One anecdote recalls how the architect's mother would allow the landlady of the Railway Tavern to draw water from the Calsay Seat well in the hope that diluted whisky would do her patrons less harm than the neat variety.

The Misses Leslie decided that what was left of the Lands of Calsayseat might as well give way to 'hard-hearted granite' and the money received put to charitable uses. A feuing plan was drawn up for remaining portions of Berryhillock and in April 1884 the Town Council approved the suggestion of Messrs Jenkins & Marr, architects, acting for the sisters, that two new streets be laid out; Leslie Terrace running south from the Powis Terrace bridge alongside the Denburn Valley Railway, and Calsayseat Road running west from just beyond Split-the-Wind to form a junction with Leslie

Leslie Place, now Nos 596-654 George Street. The former Split-the-Wind kirk is on the left.

The last house in the first section of Leslie Terrace, completed in 1884.
Calsayseat Road is to the right.

Terrace. The Misses Leslie must
have drawn a sigh of relief when
the magistrates approved the
use of their family names. In
spite of their protests, Leslie
Place had been 'discontinued'
earlier that year by the Council
and incorporated into North
Broadford, soon itself to be annexed in its turn when the cottages became Nos 596 -654
George Street. In October of 1884,
the Council gave approval for
three further streets. The first
was a continuation of Leslie Terrace southwards beyond the
junction with Calsayseat Road,
thus explaining why neighbouring houses across this junction,
each with a distinctive granite
ball finial, bear the dates 1884
and 1885. The remaining two

The start of the 1885 extention to Leslie Terrace.

'Hard-hearted granite'. Contrasting stonework in Lamond Place.
Note the wallhead gables.

streets, forming a reverse L-shape between Calsayseat Road and Leslie Terrace were enterprisingly given the names Jamaica Street and Lamond Place, recalling the old family plantation and its owners. It must have been agreed that combinations and permutations of 'Leslie' and 'Powis' were temporarily exhausted (though Leslie Road was yet to appear on the scene). Miss Lamond Leslie who had been given her maternal grandparents surname, and who was then eighty-five, must have been delighted. This little backwater has a mix of villas and new housing in Calsayseat Road, distinctive flatted properties in Leslie Terrace and tenements in Jamaica Street and Lamond Place, from where one can look across to Berryden, once the western-most edge of Calsayseat.

In 1888 the surviving Leslie sisters gifted the Split-the-Wind site to the Church of Scotland, not without returning to the old routine and ordaining that the church there be named 'Powis'. Some years passed before sufficient funds were raised to build the new kirk, but by the early 1890s, the Souttars

The Rev Dr John Duncan.

had been succeeded at Calsay Seat House by the last tenant before demolition, the remarkable Reverend John Duncan. Duncan's teetotal susceptibilities were not offended by the proximity of an inn. The Railway Tavern, the old 'Coffin' had become a mason's workshop.

John Duncan was one of the most outstanding ministers in the city's history. As a young man he had been chaplain to Scottish workmen building the Szécheny Chain Bridge over the Danube at Budapest, engineered by a Scot, Adam Clark. In Aberdeen he became minister of the Bool Road or Albion Street Congregational Church - the Ragged Kirk. The Bool Road, long buried under the Beach Boulevard, was Aberdeen's most notorious den of vice but Duncan did much to reform the area. His talents as a great temperance preacher and a brilliant exponent of the Doric were appreciated and he filled the church to overflowing. He had a splendid collection of anecdotes which regretfully he never got down on paper. As he argued with much truth, 'Cauld print is a trying thing.' By the time he was living at Calsay Seat, however, he and his congregation had already moved to the new Trinity Congregational Church in the Shiprow which a century later was destined to become an extension to Aberdeen Maritime Museum. But we have wandered far into Calsayseat and the Gallowgate-head beckons us back.

This postcard from the early 1930s captures the village atmosphere of Mounthooly. The quaint house with the wallhead gable, left, and its neighbour with the chubby dormers, stood alone for some years, before the tenements to the right went up in the 1870s. The cottage beyond the cul-de-sac has gone, and its neighbour, only just visible, is now the Mounthooly Newsagent. Michie the grocer is the first shop in Causewayend, extreme left, while extreme right is Adam & Craigmile the fruiteres.

32

Chapter 3

At Mounthooly

To be sold at Mounthooly...that large house with an extensive garden adjoining...The houses are substantial and but lately built. The situation is dry and well-aired.

Aberdeen Journal, August 29, 1810

By the late eighteenth century, the name of the little settlement that straddled both sides of the Spital Road just beyond the Gallowgate-head had probably even more variations than Footdee; Mount Hodey, Mount Hily, Mount Hilie, Mount Hooley, Mount Heillie and Mountheely were all on offer. And as with Kittybrewster, there are rival theories as to the origins of the word Mounthooly. The most favoured explanation is that it is a corruption of Holy Mount, the allusion being to the Spital Hill where St Peter's Hospital for aged and infirm clergy had a shadowy existence centuries ago, and whose site is now covered by a part of St Peter's Cemetery. Gaelic place-name enthusiasts, on the other hand, may opt for 'a wooded hill' from *monadh*, hill and *coille*, wood which, when pronounced quickly together, sound rather like Mounthooly. These theories are brought into question by the fact that Mounthooly is low-lying. To make sense of it one would have to assume that the name merely indicates the road to the holy mount or the wooded hill. Mounthoolygate, in fact.

The opening of the Ellon or North Turnpike, with its King Street home stretch, may not have caused the ancient Old Aberdeeen-Spital road to be bypassed any more than it already was. Many country folk from further north, who would now take the turnpike, had already been using an alternative route of great antiquity via the Links and the embryonic Park Road. Those travelling to Aberdeen from Old Aberdeen would continue to use the Spital route as the handiest, though it presented the drawbacks of a hill and a marsh.

Mounthooly, however, did find itself caught in something of a pincer movement between the Aberdeenshire Canal which flowed past the Spital end, and where a bridge was built to carry the road over the canal, and the Inverurie Turnpike which came through from Causewayend at the Gallowgate-head end. One of the arguments put forward by the Staats Forbes consortium in favour of the George Street route was that it would save the cost of purchasing houses at the Gallowgate-head, presumably for demolition. With the reinstatement of the Causewayend route, however, such savings were not to be and a little group of buildings sitting near the centre of the Gallowgate-head were demolished to allow the turnpike to run into the Gallowgate-head at its specified width. The peace and calm of the little settlement must have been seriously disrupted by bridge-building and canal excavating at one end, and demolition and road-building at the other.

For much of the eighteenth century Mounthooly's dwellings would have been straw-thackit cottages. The quaint house with the wallhead gable and its neighbour, shown left in the photograph on page 32 were probably the first 'good' houses to be built. The quaint house, later Nos 1-3 Mounthooly, may possibly pre-date the turnpike. For many years during the earlier part of the nineteenth century it was the home and the surgery of James Philip, MD as well as his dispensary, for in those days doctors dispensed their own medicines. Earlier still, in the 1780s, Dr William Chalmers, Professor of Medicine at King's and physician in Aberdeen, had a chemist's shop in Mounthooly, where it was the apprentice's task to take down the shutters every morning. (Completing an apprenticeship was the only means of qualifying as a doctor when neither King's nor Marischal College offered a regular course in medicine). Could this have been the place?

Dr William Chalmers. A detail from John Kay's caricature, 'The Seven Wise Men'. Courtesy, the University of Aberdeen.

Wherever the location of Dr Chalmer's shop, we do know that a chemist's was located at the quaint house was for most of its existence. The 1890 valuation roll shows that the ground floor shop on the left of the photograph, No 1 Mounthooly, was a druggist's, to use the word then in vogue, run by James Spence. Miss Ingram, a milliner, also had her business there. Within a few years, the druggist's had also become the Mounthooly Post Office, and continued to be run as a joint chemist and sub-post office down the years until 1960 when the then proprietors of the business, George Mackay and his wife, Jean, had to make way for the roundabout. Mitchell and Muil the bakers were long-standing tenants next door at No 3. The neighbouring, taller and probably slightly later tenement with the chubby dormers Nos 5 - 7 (though Mounthooly street numbers change about), would have been a building of some class when Miss Beattie offered lodgings there in 1828. Others who had apartments included Samuel Clark, a linen manufacturer, in residence for thirty years from the 1820s, Harry Forbes, late of Grenada, Mrs Saunders, Joseph Wishart, organ builder, and by the 1850s, Miss Balfour, straw hat maker. (Although Miss Ingram was based for a time at No 1, there seems to have been a later tradition of milliners at No 5. In the 1890s, these were the Misses Wilson and Mrs Sime). No 7 had long been a shop run by Mrs Bain, merchant in the 1890s, while in modern times, Jeannie Forbes ran a newsagent's there and was succeeded by John H. Junor, who also served the community as a bookie's runner.

In the 1850 Bird's Eye View by George Washington Wilson overleaf, we can see other dwellings in what is now the Canal Place cul-de-sac, standing behind the two early houses. A pleasant rural hinterland had been created here between the canal and Causewayend, removed from the hustle and bustle of the turnpikes, yet not too far from the city centre. This seemed an ideal spot to build houses of the superior sort. On 27 December 1809, the *Aberdeen Journal* was advertising:

> To let at Mountheely, that large house fronting the street presently possessed by Mrs Mitchell of Thainston, consisting of dining room, drawing room, two parlours, six bedrooms, kitchen, wash-house, three cellars, garrets and several office houses and a large garden in front of the house. Also that neat house in the back ground fronting the Canal presently occupied by J. Forbes, merchant. Both houses have the use of a pump well. Apply to Mrs Henderson the proprietor at Mountheely.

Because the row of Mounthooly tenements was not then complete, 'that large house' was able to 'front the street', and have a large garden to the fore as well. It is interesting that in 1809 this house - advertised incidentally as 'fit either for a town or country residence' - was tenanted by Mrs Mitchell of Thainston. Her family's seat was near Inverurie - not the extant building designed by Archibald Simpson and now a hotel, but an eighteenth century

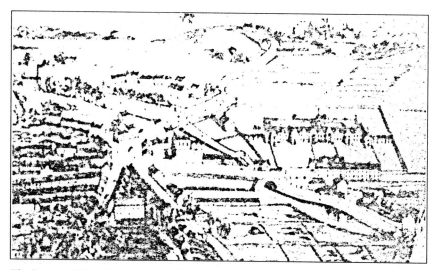

The large building bottom left, is the Porthill Factory and the open space above it, the Gallowgate-head. Beyond the latter are the two oldest Mounthooly tenements, and behind them, the houses of the Canal Place cul-de-sac. Across the gap is Canal Street. The palatial building, right, is the East Poorhouse. Below it the canal flows under the Nelson Street Bridge. The Spital winds uphill to Old Aberdeen, top right. From George Washington Wilson's Bird's Eye View, 1850.

mansion built by Sir Andrew Mitchell, British ambassador to Prussia. Thanks to the Inverurie turnpike and the option of the Causewayend approach, this Mounthooly hinterland enjoyed a brief period as a desirable and convenient place for gentry living in the Garioch to have their townhouses. However Mrs Mitchell was soon off to Dee Street which was also very new, and with Union Street completed and the city centre moving west, even more fashionable. Less than a year later this same 'large house' with its 'extensive garden adjoining' was offered for sale along with 'two convenient houses with large bleachgreens fronting the Canal, presently occupied by Mrs Captain Fyfe and Mrs Col. Murray'.

Whatever the fate of the homes of the officers' wives, by New Year's Day, 1812 Mrs Henderson had still not sold 'that large house', which she now again offered for rent 'in whole or in flats', as well as 'a small convenient house', possibly the 'neat house' where Alex Duguid, clothier, appears to have replaced J. Forbes as tenant. The spelling in the advertisement has stabilised at Mounthooly. It seems that regardless of their attractions, these houses were changing owners or tenants fairly rapidly, just as at the Gallowgate-head. With the canal so near, there may have been a particular reason for the disenchantment. A contemporary news item in the *Aberdeen Journal* reveals that the body of a new born male child was found in the canal a little above Mounthooly. 'It had apparently been in the water for some days,' it reports. 'No discovery has been made of the unnatural parents.' This stretch of water, close to the increasingly densely populated new streets offered a convenient if desperate way of disposing of an unwanted baby. It is impossible to tell how many newly-born infants met their end in the canal.

The cul-de-sac would also have been affected by increasing industrialisation all around. Because of the time taken to go through the eleven locks between Kittybrewster and Waterloo Quay, passengers disembarked at the Kittybrewster boathouse and this final section of the canal was used solely by the goods barges. When in 1811, for example, a house at Mounthooly occupied by James Diack went on the market, a prime selling point was that the ground that went with it ran 100 feet along Mounthooly and stretched back 200 feet along the Canal. The advertisement concluded: 'The premises are well adapted for a timber yard'. Such a yard was subsequently built at Mounthooly and during the canal era, it would have been ideally sited for loading the barges with wood destined for Inverurie. Other products regularly shipped at Mounthooly included fertiliser to enrich the fields of the Garioch, supplied from 1830 by Messrs Barry, Henry and Co. (Cook came much later on the scene). This company not only manufactured machinery, but at that time had a side-line in fertilisers, made by crushing bones at their premises nearby at Lochside, later Loch Street. So although Mounthooly had a wharf which was the principal town station for the canal, it was essentially a goods wharf, and residents would have experienced much noise and bustle, with barges tying up to load, and carts rumbling past.

By the late nineteenth century the occupants of these genteel 'back' houses must have been overwhelmed by industry. William Fiddes's sawmill had taken over the timber yard - this was before the move to Torry - and the versatile James Fraser's Balmoral Soap Powder Works and Aberdeen Margarine Factory was nearby. He made blacking too. A small slaughterhouse at the far end of the cul-de-sac made its presence felt. It was nothing more than a dilapidated wooden shed divided in two, one half a killing booth, the other, holding cattle awaiting slaughter. Refuse was thrown into a 'large offensive midden' while overflowing into it was a cesspool used to collect waste blood. Filth was everywhere and there was no water. The yard, unpaved and thick with mud in wet weather, was bounded by a mere wooden rail offering a ringside view to idlers. In 1883, Dr Simpson, the city's medical officer of health, recommended 'that the Slaughterhouse at Canal Place, Mounthooly be discontinued'. There was also the ubiquitous granite yard. By the end of the nineteenth century there were about forty yards within half a mile radius of Mounthooly, providing a constant chorus of clinking hammers.

Some of the industrial activity of the cul-de-sac would have been hidden when the tenements completing the row made their appearance in the 1870s. They were home to numerous tenants, nine families at No 9 and No 11, ten at No 13. Forbes 'Fobbie' Wright the hairdresser had the ground floor shop at No 9a, which was once the funeral parlour of Ben Cormack who himself had succeeded earlier generations of undertakers there. On the ground floor of the last of these tall tenements was a grocer's and newsagent's No 13a, run by Mrs Ella McKay, and after the war by Donald Archibald. This whole stretch of Mounthooly, and round the corner into Causewayend was owned by Dr John Wight of Viewfield House, and was factored by his kindred at Messrs Wight and Aitken's Dickensian office at 3 King Street.

After Nos 13-13a there was a gap and Canal Place, allowed access to the houses of the cul-de-sac and to the various industries located there. As the twentieth century progressed, these had changed in character since the days of the shambles and the sawmill. It was here that Munro's Transport Co started in a large Nissen-style hut, with R Hutchison, the Hutcheon Street scrap firm taking over, followed by Tupperware. Beyond the cul-de-sac and back now in the front row were two old cottages, the nearer of

The Newsagent at No 13a Mounthooly. This tenement building was the last before the Canal Place cul-de-sac. Courtesy, City of Aberdeen-Planning Division.

which, the low house in the postcard, No 27, thought to date from around 1770, was, by the late nineteenth century, a little dairy farm with byres behind, run by Alex Ingram. Later it housed five tenants. No 29, only just visible, was once tenanted by a shoemaker. It later became Barry's Cafe, where you could get a lovely meal to take away for 2/-, providing you brought your own plate. It was run by a Mrs Margaret Cowe in the 1930s, and by Mrs Barbara Thomson in the 1950s. Anne Brand (Mrs Logan) who lived nearby in Canal Street remembers its speciality; delicious home-made chips produced from a stove in the back shop.

Some of the little straw-thackit biggings on the east side of Mounthooly, had been demolished by 1835 to make way for the first John Knox Church which faced out across Mounthooly. A few remained as shown below but all had gone by the end of the nineteenth century when a railing was put round the church and the area was planted with a neat triangular border of trees.

Mounthooly in the 1830s, looking towards the Gallowgate. The first John Knox kirk is on the left, behind the thatched cottage. Courtesy, John Knox's Church.

Many readers will see in their mind's eye the present JohnKnox's Church which dates from 1911, towering over a group of little shops that sat in front of it, virtually on the pavement. Mrs Muriel Slessor, brought up in the Sunnybank area, and with her husband Alex, a lifelong member of John Knox's, remembers Adam & Craigmile, florists and fruiterers round at No

Nos 2 and 4 Mounthooly. The A & A Douglas sign can be made out with Nos 6-8 side on. John Knox's Kirk towers behind. From the 1954 watercolour by I W Davidson.

2, a better class of shop, she recalls, which sold lovely strawberries. Adam & Craigmile were also rose growers, with nurseries at Fernielea and Upper Rosewell. Next door, was a little shop, for a time Watson the shoemaker, sometimes a coal store, but often boarded up. No 4 was traditionally a butcher's, latterly, A & A Douglas. This little group was built on that very 'piece of angular ground at the Gallowgate-head of Aberdeen', which so long ago had been sold by Robert Connon to William Wildgoose. It was owned for many years in more modern times by Mr and Mrs Antonio d'Alessandro.

Nos 6-8 were round the corner back towards Mounthooly, alongside the church. A weaver and four families lived here in the nineteenth century. Later, Philips, the tailor, had the ground floor shop. Steps led down to this

40

Nos 6-8 Mounthooly at right angles to the church. Note the pestle and mortar outside the chemist's at No 1 Mounthooly, extreme left. Courtesy John Knox's Church.

shop, unlike Adam & Craigmile where steps led up to the entrance. There was a sweet shop here later, and in the 1950s, Canale's ice cream shop. This little group would not have looked so curious when originally built. Old John Knox's Church faced across Mounthooly and Nos 6-8 would have been in the same line. The new kirk of 1911 was built at right angles to the shops, towering over them. 'It's almost as if it was anticipated even then that they might be demolished one day,' says the Reverend Laurie Gordon, minister of John Knox's.

There were many other shops, all around Mounthooly, in Causewayend and the Gallowgate and they will be recalled in Chapter Eleven.

41

Part Two

Canalside

The Mount Pleasant Arch

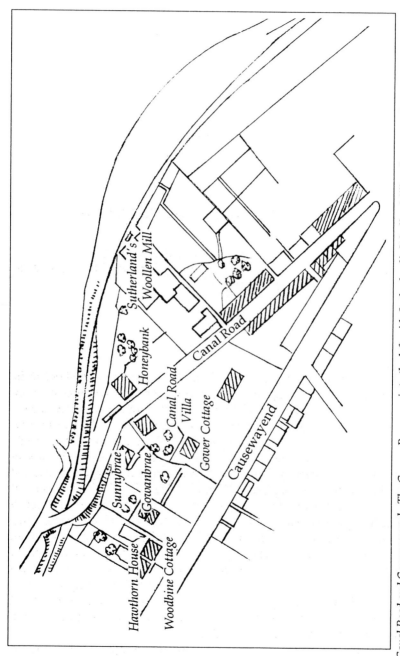

Canal Road and Causewayend. The Gowan Brae area is to the left with Sutherland's Woollen Mill at the top. Milne's Preserving Works later occupied this site.

Chapter 4

Canal Road and Izzy Masson's Brae

Canal Road: From Causewayend to Froghall.
Aberdeen Post Office Directory, 1854 - 55

When the Causewayend fork of the Inverurie turnpike was laid out at the beginning of the nineteenth century, the section of the old highway between the Gallowgate-head and Froghall, robbed of much of its *raison d'etre.*, underwent an identity crisis. Compared with the new road it was narrow and hilly, a poor thing. No one was going to tackle it as an alternative route to the Garioch for old times' sake. Unlike Canal Street across on the northwest bank of the waterway, it had not the advantage of being newly laid out under the prestigious auspices of King's College. Unlike Mounthooly, it could not expect the regular passage of folk from a neighbouring community like the Spital *en route* to town, endowing the area with some life. True, it gave access to and from Froghall and Sunnyside, as it still does, but with only two-three cottages at Froghall, the farm at Sunnyside and a couple of country mansions, these areas were not great centres of population. Moreover the gentry at Powis House, once regular users of the old highway, now had a road through their policies which connected with the turnpike at Berryhillock. (This estate road became the old Kittybrewster Road, and in its turn was supplanted by Bedford Road).

As if being left in limbo wasn't bad enough, the old highway had no name of its own. The blanket name of Causewayend was often used, for the old settlement had flanked the highway, thus causing confusion with the turnpike; sometimes it was called Canalside like everything else around the canal, from Elmfield, 'a dwelling house on Canalside, half-a-mile above Mounthooly' (it was, in fact, within the Spital Lands), right round to Canal Street on the opposite bank, which was also known as Canalside, Mounthooly. But, unlike other stretches of the highway, which went into oblivion, this section survived. The few cottages that flanked it, part of the original Causewayend community, must have bestowed some vitality. The soap manufacturer Robert Davidson, the owner of Elmfield House, situated roughly in the middle of what became Elmbank Terrace, also played a part as saviour of the old road. In the 1820s, he moved his business from Duncan's Court in the Gallowgate to new premises in Hutcheon Street, but to reach either factory he must have passed down the old highway every day and been aware of its potential. It was probably he who persuaded his nephew and namesake, the electrical genius Robert Davidson, of whom more anon, to set up there, proving that the old road, a few minutes walk from the town, yet virtually in the country, was a good place to live and to develop one's business.

By the time young Robert Davidson arrived there, the old highway had recently gained the imaginative name of Canal Road, running 'from Causewayend to Froghall', inevitably causing confusion with Canal Street across the waterway, and Canal Place, the cul-de-sac behind Mounthooly. Davidson would have found himself surrounded by the nurseries shown on page 16, the nearest of which, possibly owned by Adam and Alexander Rannie, stretched halfway up Canal Road. Across the canal, James Smith had nurseries which in time would bestride both sides of Froghall Lane, now Froghall Terrace, while in 1848, 'James Cocker, gardener' set up at Sunnypark, next door to Smith's Froghall Nurseries. The Cockers, later famous for their roses, specialised in 'all kinds of stove and greenhouse plants for general use' as well as flowers for bouquets and herbaceous plants in their 'extensive and perfectly appointed nursery'. Across Mounthooly, in the Nelson Street-North Street wedge, was the old-established nursery of James Roy, who would later move to Polmuir, whilst out at Kittybrewster, Messrs Cardno and Darling, had some sixty acres under cultivation, 'including the various flowers sought after by bees'. Little wonder that at one time, the younger Robert Davidson turned his talents to horticulture.

By the mid-nineteenth century he had developed a number of businesses at his premises. Others had followed suit and Canal Road had made the transition from a once-important highway to a street full of life and industry, with a distinct personality of its own. The 1851 census returns reveal a mix of residents, gentlemen industrialists like Davidson, and skilled artisans. No 10 at the lower end, for example, was tenanted by William Christie flax mill overseer. Working class folk, cotton spinners, flax spinners and yarn winders may well have occupied cottages dating back to the highway era. Engineers, clerks and carters, as usual many of country stock, came later.

In John Tallis's Plan of Aberdeen *circa* 1854, the house of Honeybank sits at the top of Canal Road with the woollen mill of A Sutherland & Sons, set up there in 1850, (address still 'Canal Road, Causewayend') immediately to the south. The Sutherlands were 'worsted spinners, hosiers and girth manufacturers', with their warehouse - a shop and showroom rather than a storeroom in the modern sense - in Black's Buildings, where their business, like that of the notable draper William 'Raggy' Morrison, had originated. The Sutherlands occupied Nos 1, 2 and 3 Black's Buildings where Andrew Sutherland Snr and his son also made their home. Many of us can recall the place as Aberdeen's most notorious slum, but this tall row of buildings had some style and distinction in its early days. A few years later the Sutherlands were living in the west end, in a fine townhouse in Bon Accord Square designed by Archibald Simpson, so the Canal Road mill must have been doing well. In the early 1860s, however, Andrew Jnr is living over the shop in Canal Road. The cause of this comedown may have been a recession in the trade; it may have been that Sutherland's warehouse was damaged by the same fire at Black's Buildings that caused William Morrison to flit to the St Nicholas Street-Netherkirkgate corner where his business gained ever-lasting fame, at least in Aberdeen and twal mile roon. Whatever the cause, the woollen mill went out of business and was taken over by Thomas Watson, rag merchant.

By 1876, Sutherland and Watson had been succeeded by Alexander Milne & Son, manufacturers of preserved provisions who had started two years earlier in a small way, making jam in Young Street, one of three little streets - the others were Innes Street and Berry Street - near the foot of the Gallowgate, opposite the Porthill Factory. The jam market flourished and increasing trade demanded larger premises, hence the move to Canal Road with its on-the-spot source of supply from the surrounding nurseries. The firm continued to grow and the old mill was improved and much enlarged. So busy were Milnes that they set up another large factory in Wales Street, where jam and marmalade as well as preserved fish and meats, soups and jellies were produced for the firm's 'immense trade …with foreign and colonial markets' and where the tinsmith's shop made all their cans. Canal Road jam was for home consumption. The Milnes employed a workforce of over 250. Our illustration shows their Preserved Provision Works at 36-

The Canal Road Provision Works of Alexander Milne & Sons, an illustration reproduced from 'Scotland of Today', 1889. A train on the GNSR Waterloo line is glimpsed in the background, puffing towards Kittybrewster. Permission, City of Aberdeen-Arts and Recreation Division - Library Services.

42 Canal Road. Alexander Milne Snr was another who lived over the shop and the smart house to the fore was likely his. The premises glimpsed to the right may have been part of Robert Davidson's terrain. His home at No 32 was about half way down, and he owned the neighbouring five cottages below. James Minty, an inspector with the old Commissioners of Police, responsible for paving, lighting and cleansing in those days, lived for many years at No 16. Minty too was a local landlord and his tenants at Nos 8 - 14 included two lamplighters, a carpet weaver, a plasterer and a blind combmaker.

At the foot of the road near the site of the present Causewayend School, Greyfriars Church ran a school established by its minister, the Reverend Abercromby Gordon, a tireless pioneer of education in Aberdeen. The junction of Canal Road and Causewayend formed a miniature Split-the-

Wind, with its own 'Coffinie', a diminution of its counterpart at Split-the-Wind. Beside it was one of the ferlies of the locality, a menagerie owned by old Peter Hercules, 'Herkless' in the local argot. The Davidsons and the Greyfriars scholars would have able to smell it. In the *Book of Powis* William Smith writes:

> Peter's establishment was a standing marvel and attraction to young folk from far and near. It was to them a veritable Noah's Ark, and contained all manner of animals and creeping things, from a wild untamed golloch, to mice, rats, cats, dogs, ferrets, squirrels, hawks, larks and so on in an ascending scale of importance and magnitude till the tame but chained fox was reached. For a brief period the menagerie gloried in the possession of a mangy wolf of anything but ferocious aspect. But a wolf was a wolf.

Time wore on, and a colourful mix of the industrialised and the rural lived side by side in Canal Road. By the 1890s the 'Herkless' menagerie was replaced by a 'Fire Engine Depot and Privy' at the mini Split-the-Wind. Inspector Minty would have been able to keep an eye on them on his way to work at the Police Offices and Writing Chambers in St Nicholas Street - Woolworth's later appeared on that site. The fire engine was probably a handcart. The depot later became a scaffies' store.

The miniature Split-the-Wind at the junction of Causewayend and Canal Road.

A bird stuffer, William Center, lived in the cottages on the west side in Davidson's day and there was a salmon fisher and several families of hawkers, and a smithy further up. The hawkers were there for many years, and coming to modern times, Muriel Slessor recalls them as nice folk. Mrs Townsley was a well-remembered matriarch, not afraid to tick off her grown up sons, if she thought it necessary. There was a variety of houses in Canal Road; small tenements, larger ones near the foot of the brae, houses that you went down steps to enter. Some of the cottages such as Meldrum Cottage and Admiral Cottage may have dated from the old highway days. Muriel Slessor recalls Rowan Cottage, 'a lovely little house half way down.' Norah Morrison (Mrs Fairless) who spent her childhood in the area recalls the houses, crowded with children but all spotless inside. She remembers gypsy caravans too, and a little carnival which would occasionally come to a patch of ground about half way down. She queued for coal on the same spot during the General Strike in 1926.

Apart from the carnival, there were other sporadic entertainments for Canal Roaders. A roller skating craze in Aberdeen replaced the earlier fad for menageries and Canal Road boasted one of the first in the city, the Bon Accord Skating Rink which opened in 1909. Its existence was short-lived, but not as brief as that of its successor, the Grand Picture Palace, which opened in the former rink premises in 1912, and which we can assume was neither grand nor palatial. Variety shows and illustrated songs were the order of the day or at least of the night, and though seats were modestly priced at 1d, 2d and 3d it lasted less than a year. Much later there was a bowling green on the east side.

Plasterers and builders, joiners and slaters and a coal merchant were to be found at the foot of the road. In the 1880s, the Belmont Granite Yard of Gauld & Third occupied an acre just up from Causewayend School, where monuments, crosses, tablets, columns and polished pillars, all in the finest Aberdeen granites, awaiting export, were a familiar sight. John Third, sole partner by the 1890s employed a workforce of fifty and sent his memorials 'of rare beauty and splendid substance' to every quarter of the globe.

Another great exporting firm was next door. The agricultural engineer Robert G. Garvie had set up in business at the Hardgate Iron Works in 1890 and by 1917 was established at No 1a, later No 2 Canal Road. This firm of agricultural implement makers and millwrights were in business for over half a century and their memory remains fresh. The Garvie's *forte* was the manufacture of threshing mills for export and the firm maintained personal contact with customers far and wide, in Eastern Europe, North America, Africa, Asia, the Irish Republic and Ulster. The firm's expertise was appreciated at the highest levels. In 1969 Donald Garvie, the third genera-

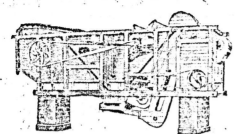

"GARVIE" THRESHING MACHINES

WE HAVE SPECIALISED
IN THE MANUFACTURE
OF THRESHERS FOR 40
YEARS, & HAVE TO-DAY
THE LARGEST & BEST
EQUIPPED THRESHER
WORKS IN SCOTLAND.

WE ARE EXHIBITING, AS USUAL AT THE HIGHLAND SHOW
WHICH IS TO BE HELD IN ABERDEEN FROM JUNE 18th to 21st.
We will have on view a full range of the most up-to-date BALL-BEAR-
ING THRESHERS, and we cordially invite you to visit our stand.

R. G. GARVIE & SONS, 2 Canal Road, ABERDEEN

An R G Garvie advertisement circa 1935.

tion head of the firm, undertook a three month tour of the Far East, one of a team of United Nations' experts, advising on food production, cropping and storage.

Garvie's also had an interesting sideline that had nothing to do with agricultural machinery. They produced wooden heads for golf clubs by a novel duplicating system. (An older branch of the family, James Garvie & Sons, were well known cabinet-makers, based at 55 Rose Street, the site of the old Bridewell, in the late nineteenth century. Working with wood was in the Garvie blood).

Back near the top of the brae, Alexander Milne had given up the preserves business by the 1920s and the production of black puddings, mealies and potted heed had replaced the jam, though on a small part of the old site. 'I can still see the pudding skins hanging up,' recalls Alex Slessor. It was a one man business run by 'Puddin' Allan after the First World War. He lived in the Spital near St Peter's Gate. At a later date, Mrs Isobel Donaldson recalls a favourite errand in childhood, being sent to buy a dozen mealie puddings from George Birnie, a successor to 'Puddin'. Before demolition, the factory, little more than a wooden shed, was occupied by a tile fixer. Honeybank, No 52, at the top had been the home of a medical student, David Lawson in the 1870s, and had gone over to multi-tenancy by the 1890s. William Collie the painter and two other families lived there. Norah Morrison remembers that latterly it was the home of the Mutch family.

Below Honeybank was Gowan Brae. In the older census returns it appears as part of Causewayend. The street directories described it as 'a group of dwelling houses at the north end of Causewayend, right hand side' which is not very helpful. The 1869 Ordnance Survey comes to one's aid, showing a scattering of cottages that climbed up to meet Canal Road beside the railway bridge at Froghall. In fact it formed the base of a long, thin triangle, with Causewayend and Canal Road meeting at the apex. The folk of Gowan Brae - the 'gowany parks' beloved of Cassie-end bairns - were a mixed bunch. While the area was still developing its rural setting combined with its handiness for the city had attracted some superior houses. During the 1870s, for example Woodbine Cottage was the home of William Ligertwood, a master mason employing ten men and three boys. Yet it was only yards away from Greens and Gower Cottages which housed numerous working class families. These houses, along with Hawthorn House were on the straight. The little dairy farm of Gowan Brae, which took its name from the brae, was about half way up while Sunnybrae and Canal Road Villa were nearer the junction with Canal Road.

There had long been a tradition of dairymen or cowfeeders as they used to be called in Causewayend. The names of two early nineteenth century ones have come down to us. One was John Law. Another called Peters faced a great crisis in January 1834. His cow had refused food for three days so:

A mash of malt was given to her and the result was that the contents of her stomach fermented and swelled to a fearful size. Mr Barclay, the Cow Leech, was sent for. He made an incision and opened her stomach and there was taken out as much undigested food as would have filled a wheel barrow, The animal is now eating her food and recovering rapidly.

Hopefully no such dramas confronted Causewayend's - or rather Gowan Brae 's best known dairy farmer of all - Izzy Masson.

From the latter part of the nineteenth century until well into modern times, locals bought their milk from the dairy farm on Gowan Brae. In the 1870s a family of five lived there, the dairyman, Charles Masson, his wife, their son William and two daughters Isabella and Elizabeth, or Izzy and Lizzy as everyone called them. In addition to the farmhouse the little farm toon consisted of a couple of byres and three small parks. In 1896, however, the Town Council decided to construct a through road at Gowan Brae, linking Causewayend-Powis Place at their junction and Canal Road. This new road must have taken a sizeable chunk from the farm for William, who had inherited the property by this time, was paid £275 for loss of his ground,

Izzy Masson's Brae.

a fair sum in those days. He had become a pattern maker and draughtsman, and it was Izzy assisted by the red-headed Lizzy who ran the farm. Gowan Brae vanished. The new road, an extension of Fraser Place, is not named as such, but can be identified by the Brown and Root building on one side, and a bathroom centre on the other, at least at time of writing. Gowan Brae Farm became 49 Fraser Place but it was rarely called that. It was 'Izzy Masson's' and the new road became known locally as Izzy Masson's Brae, as it remains to this day.

Izzy's herd of about twelve cows grazed across in Froghall in three parks beside the Jute Works ponds, the site of a BT carpark these days. Perhaps the Massons had always used these parks, but perhaps the loss of land at Gowan Brae compelled Izzy to find pastures new. Whatever the reason, a particular routine was followed at milking time. When Norah Morrison, who lived near the Tarry Briggie, the railway bridge at Froghall, came home from school she would find the cows standing at the gate of the field waiting to be milked. She opened the gate and the herd walked along Froghall Terrace, on to the bridge, and then down the brae, and in through the double gates to be milked in the byre by Izzy. Norah would help, carrying the cans into the dairy where customers would be waiting with their jugs. With no refrigerators local people might buy milk twice a day. Muriel Slessor recalls how threatening the cows could look to a little girl if you met them on the

Tarry Briggie looking across to Froghall.

road. She remembers Izzy's son Charlie from schooldays. He took over as dairyman, was a familiar figure about the place and was associated latterly with the marts. 'He was very nice,' she recalls, very like Izzy.' He remained at 49 Fraser Place until the 1960s.

In modern times, Canal Road has suffered another identity crisis. Everything that is remembered so vividly about the street has gone. Robert Davidson's premises vanished not long after his death, and it could be that part of this area was used by the Spring Garden engineering firm of W McKinnon & Co as a pipe storage yard in the inter-war years. It appears enigmatically in a splendid engraving of their Spring Garden Works, which the firm used for many years in their advertisements and letterheads. In order to show the plant as a neatly contained whole, however, Mounthooly had to be omitted! Canal Road is identifiable by the train puffing along the Waterloo line in the distance.

Before the last war, the whole central area of the east side became a Corporation Transport Depot. In the mid-1950s the long-established local firm of J G Barrack took over a sizeable part of this area for their haulage business, and remained there for nearly twenty years until they were acquired by the oil service firm, Seaforth Maritime, in the early 1970s. The haulage company later became Seaforth Transport, and the yard, now

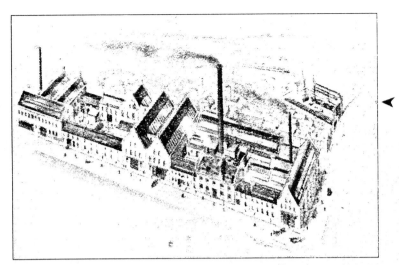

A detail from McKinnon's standard advertisement. The Canal Road pipe storage yard is arrowed.

shared with a bus company, remains in use for transport engineering as part of the Seaforth Logistics Ltd set-up at Canal Road.

By the 1970s all the Canal Road houses had been demolished and the old highway north now has a cul-de-sac at its Mounthooly end, created to relieve pressure on the roundabout. Access is via Froghall Terrace or from

Canal Road 1995. The same area a hundred years ago is shown on page 48.

Causewayend via Izzy Masson's Brae. On the east side, apart from the transport yard, there is a motor tyre supplier at the top, and a transport social club and a car showroom at the lower end. There is nothing opposite, bar a filling station which really belongs to Causewayend. Knowing something of Canal Road's history, one can stand at the bottom of the brae and get a faint sense of the old narrow rural highway. But as one walks up towards Froghall, a feeling of emptiness prevails. Izzy Masson's Brae remains, but in total anonymity. The site of the farm is encompassed by the yard behind the bathroom centre. Only the old walls, and, across the way, a tangle of bushes where Honeybank once stood, give a glimmering of a earlier, very different way of life.

'...where Honeybank once stood'.

Chapter 5

Robert Davidson...'the oldest living electrician'

He applied his ingenious mind to many branches of industry, and in every case he turned his investigations to practical account.

Obituary: In Memoriam, 1894

In 1894, when the building of Powis Church was at last getting underway at Split-the-Wind, the remarkable Robert Davidson of Canal Road, the pioneer of electric traction, had reached the end of a long life. He was born in 1804, the son of William Davidson, grocer, wine merchant and burgess whose shop at 44 Broad Street was opposite the entrance to old Marischal College. A pupil at two of Lord Byron's old schools, Bodsy Bower's in Longacre and the Grammar School in Schoolhill, Robert entered Marischal College at the age of 14 as most lads did in those days. He attended classes for the next six years, which was rather longer than usual. According to his obituary:

He devoted himself chiefly to the study of chemistry and mechanics; indeed so much attention did he pay to those sections of the curriculum that, although he was enabled to prolong his studies longer than usual, on account of the assistance he rendered one of the professors by the construction of a model engine for demonstration purposes, he failed to graduate.

There was no stigma in those days. Graduation was a formality for which a fee was paid and the 'finals' consisted of repeating answers that had been given out earlier. But it is interesting that Davidson assisted 'one of the professors' in the construction of a model engine. This was likely to have been the renowned Patrick Copland who taught Natural Philosophy (Physics) at Marischal College between 1780 and 1822. His courses were illustrated by numerous experiments, and he was reckoned to have the most complete collection of working models in the kingdom, some of which he constructed himself, some he acquired while touring on the Continent. Many remain in the care of Aberdeen University. Professor Copland was

Robert Davidson
'...*a pawky, shrewd octogenarian with a twinkle in his eye.*'

a brilliant and inspiring demonstrator all his life, though by the time Robert Davidson attended his lectures he would have been in his seventies and doubtless welcomed the assistance of a young lad with a flair for mechanics. As far as the chemistry course was concerned, Davidson studied under Professor George French MD and his successor William Henderson. Chemistry in relation to medicine, pharmacy, agriculture and manufacturing was taught, much of which would serve him well in later life.

After leaving Marischal College he served his time at his father's shop but found the grocery trade 'by no means congenial,' according to his obituarist. 'However, he soon found an outlet for his energies...' Folk brewed their own ale in those days and Robert noted that his father did a brisk trade in brewer's yeast. He carried out some successful experiments, then took the plunge and set up on his own in 1825 as a yeast brewer in Causewayend. He had continued to live in the family homes in the Guestrow and later in Drum's Lane but by 1832 was in residence in Canal Road with his mother, who had been widowed two years earlier, and his older brother William, now in charge of the Broad Street business. At this time the name Causewayend, as we know, still encompassed Canal Road, and it could have been that he had built or acquired a house beside his business premises, and both were sited from the start in what became Canal Road. And we have already speculated that his Uncle Robert might have encouraged him to set up in this area, so close to town, yet offering space for expansion.

With the yeast business proving successful, young Robert began experimenting in other branches of chemistry. With so many mills in the vicinity producing wool, wincey, linen and jute, he was inspired to set up the Aberdeen Colouring Works to produce textile dyes for this excellent market so close at hand. He had the Aberdeenshire Canal at his doorstep to provide water and, if required, to transport his dyes to the Woodside mills. Until 1834, he had been described in the street directory as a 'yeast maker' or 'yeast brewer', but that year, 'manufacturing chemist' is added, and it was as 'chemist' that he would be listed until the last entry in 1894-95.

Even closer to his premises than textile mills were the nurseries noted in Chapter Four. Surrounded by acres given over to fruit, flowers and vegetables, Davidson was prompted to put his knowledge of agricultural chemistry to good effect. He introduced a horticulture branch to the business, growing phloxes, geraniums and dahlias for Benjamin Reid whose offices were then at 94 Union Street. In the Broad Street shop William Davidson was now also styling himself 'dealer in agricultural seeds' so Robert may well have been experimenting with cereals and using the family firm as an outlet for seeds as well as yeast.

He was also in business as a file manufacturer. Yet again his studies were used to good effect. Davidson's great champion, Dr A F Anderson, notes that file sharpening required a knowledge of chemistry 'in order to manufacture the temperature-sensitive coating put on the files prior to hardening'. With a variety of industrial premises springing up around him, and tools much in use, here was another gap in the market to be filled. His file sharpening business employed three men, professionals from Sheffield. A true Aberdonian, he had put everything he learnt at Marischal College to practical use. At one point, he even worked as a dentist, making his own equipment.

There was time too for hobbies. His interest in astronomy must have been stimulated in childhood by a fine Dolland telescope that sat in the open air at the top of the west wing of Marischal College some sixty feet above the College courtyard. It was part of the equipment of a small observatory that had originally been established on the Castlehill by the 'considerable exertions' of Professor Copland. In 1797 the equipment was removed to the College where a new observatory was built by courtesy of the government who required the Castlehill site for barracks. During his student days Robert possibly used this same telescope to study the heavenly bodies, as part of his Natural Philosophy course.

Professor Patrick Copland, from a portrait in the possession of his descendants.

He built several telescopes for his personal use and at the age of twenty-four created one that was 35 ft high. Experts are pretty sure that it would have had a large mirror near the bottom and number of ladders which Davidson would have climbed to carry out his observations. It remained at the Canal Road premises for many years, fitted up on a platform. It must have been something of a local landmark, though unfortunately no illustration of it has come to light. Davidson also had an amazing collection of

Old Marischal College . The telescope can be seen on top of the tower, left.

watches 'of old and quaint design', and superb clocks including one once owned by Lord Byron which played a tune every three hours. Again, he may have been inspired by the 'high tech' clocks of the Marischal observatory which included a time-keeper with a gridiron, and an 'assistant clock' for counting seconds by the ear (it chimed every second) as well as a quadrant, and an orrery showing the movement of the planets.

His greatest fame, however, was as the inventor and builder of the first electric locomotive. He had studied electricity, magnetism and galvanism at Marischal College but the experiments he carried out in the 1830s had taken him beyond what he had learnt from Copland. By 1839 he had devised a special form of galvanic battery, and built his first electric motor. Davidson was a modest sort of chap, but a champion of his work now came forward. This was the Reverend Dr Patrick Forbes, Professor of Humanity (Latin) at King's College and lecturer there in chemistry, truly a lad o' pairts. Much impressed by Davidson's work in electromagnetism, he wrote to Michael Faraday who was also experimenting with the electric motor and

Michael Faraday.

electric current, outlining Davidson's achievements, and staking a claim for his work. Forbes expressed the hope that railroad proprietors would 'take up the subject, and be at the expense of making the experiments necessary to bring this power into operation on a great scale, which indeed would be very trifling to a company'.

In 1840, Davidson exhibited at the Mechanics Institute, and to make the public aware of his work, he was persuaded to hold an Electro-Magnetic Exhibition which he did that October at 36 Union Street. Several thousand visitors paid the 1/- admission fee and marvelled over his working models. These included a model of a locomotive carriage 'sufficient to carry two persons', a turning lathe, a small electric printing machine, an Electro-magnet, which, 'when supplied with a suitable battery will suspend a weight of several tons', and a rather sinister sounding machine 'for communicating the Electro-Magnetic shock'.

'We have enjoyed a rich treat', reported the *Aberdeen Banner*, prophesying that Electro-magnetic machinery 'will at no distant date supplant steam'. The *Aberdeen Constitutional* hoped that 'considering the number of

A model of Robert Davidson's locomotive and motor, Galvani, built by Mr Jarvis, Dorset. Courtesy, Aberdeen Gallery and Museums Collections.

accidents that are daily occurring on railways it is especially to be desired that it should supersede the steam engine'. The *Aberdeen Journal* had noted the interest of an eminent Russian scientist. Davidson now built a fully-fledged locomotive, the *Galvani*, of over 5 tons, sixteen feet long and six feet wide, and in 1842 put it through its paces on the recently opened Edinburgh and Glasgow Railway. Here, in spite of teething troubles, it reached a speed of over four miles an hour over a distance of one and a half miles. He was now persuded, under the patronage of the Royal Scottish Society of Arts, to visit the principal towns of the kingdom with his exhibition, but on the whole appears to have been a reluctant showman. His mother and brother both fussed solicitously, and it seems that he had a touch of the absent-minded professor for when he was staging his Electro-magnetic Exhibition in London in 1843, William wrote: 'I hope you are keeping your outward man in genteel order and that you will not grudge yourself some smart clothes...to the people coming in carriages it is of great importance.' And while William had recommended 'a right good dram', to keep his spirits up, his mother, anxious about the inner man, sent down fish and fine cheese.

The *Galvani* was displayed at various locations throughout Britain but alas, on reaching Perth (or Edinburgh according to some reports) on its homeward journey it was maliciously wrecked, apparently by Luddite steam engine drivers fearful of losing their livelihood.

Davidson's attempts to interest the railway companies had failed, and now his locomotive had been smashed up. These were dark days. Although he had been well off - he made a fortune from his textile dyes - he had spent a great deal of money on perfecting his machine, and a small grant of £15 awarded by the Royal Scottish Society of Arts in 1841, though welcome, had taken two years to come through. Disillusioned, he abandoned his researches. Ironically, when the GNSR's Kittybrewster to Waterloo line was laid along the old canal bed, it passed Davidson's property. This project had been in the air for years but even that did not tempt him to build a new locomotive. He continued with other experiments, however, producing a small, boat-like model of a flying machine and dabbled in photography, then in its infancy.

He lived at the same house, No 32 Canal Road, half way down on the east side, for the greater part of his life. He owned five little neighbouring houses, Nos 22 - 30, which he may have built for his workers. He enjoyed a quiet life at Canal Road, and counted among his friends John Stewart of the Aberdeen Comb Works nearby in Hutcheon Street, and Provost Gavin Hadden. He was an original member of the second Aberdeen Philosophical Society which met at the Lemon Tree Inn. For a man of science he was something of a romantic, a Jacobite sympathiser, having listened at his grandmother's knee (she was a Stuart) to tales of Bonnie Prince Charlie and the Forty-Five. As a young man he went off to explore the Continent and the field of Waterloo. As an old one, he had many reminiscences of Aberdeen in the early nineteenth century, which unfortunately, he never entrusted to pen and paper. His enthusiasm for antiques was by no means confined to clocks. He was passionately fond of music, finding house-room for no less than eighty violins, a number of organs, harmoniums, and musical boxes.

His mother died in 1854, and perhaps it was after that that Davidson, at the age of fifty, formed a liaison with her maid servant, Margaret Ross. Their daughter Mary was born in 1858, their son Robert in 1866. Robert Davidson and Margaret Ross were married in 1873.

In 1890, some fifty years after the building of the *Galvani*, the City and South of London Electric Railway was inaugurated by the Prince of Wales and electric locomotives became all the rage. Davidson 'was suddenly found to be still alive' was lionised, hailed as 'the oldest living electrician' and 'undoubtedly the first to demonstrate the possibility of electrical traction in a practical way'. A picture of him at that time, published in the *Electrician*, shows a pawky, shrewd-looking, youthful octogenarian with a twinkle in his eye. He died four years later at the age of ninety, having lived to enjoy his unexpected posterity.

Chapter 6

Canal Street and its Residents

In the country but within minutes' walk of the centre of Aberdeen.
Advertisement, Aberdeen Journal, May 8, 1883

After the Reformation, the University of King's College became feudal superior of the old croft lands around Mounthooly. King's was therefore able both to join in the early nineteenth century move to extend the town to the north, and, since indigent universities are no new thing, to fill the College kist with welcome funds. This was done by feuing out land, both in the 'industrial belt' between Causewayend and George Street, and on the unspoiled north bank of the canal, across the new Mounthooly Bridge on the old croft lands of William Umphra or Humphrie. Here, in contrast to the spasmodic development of Canal Road across the waterway, an attractive new street began to be laid out under the discerning eye of the University procurator, Dr Gilbert Gerard, and his colleagues, the Principal, Dr Roderick Macleod, Dr Alexander Dauney, Professor of Civil Law, (and uncle of the architect, Archibald Simpson), Sir Alexander Bannerman, baronet, Professor of Medicine, Dr Hugh McPherson, Professor of Greek and Mr Robert Eden Scott; the names of all the great King's College scholars of the day roll forth on the title deeds, as was the custom.

In 1808, John and Elizabeth Smith from Mount Pleasant near Peterhead secured the first feu, a spacious south-facing site, close to the Spital Road,

Mount Pleasant and neighbouring houses in 1966. Courtesy Aberdeen Journals Ltd.

'being part of the land called Humphrie's Croft, lying to the north of the new road lately made out along the bank of the Aberdeenshire Canal'. 'Within a year,' writes Mr George Gordon, a subsequent owner of this property:

> John Smith had built a commodious stone house of three storeys consisting of seven principal rooms, with a kitchen, a beer cellar and ample accommodation in the attic. The garden was planted with a variety of trees and fruit bushes and the whole area surrounded by a high stone wall with a handsome granite gateway at the south east corner of Canal Street.

John Smith named his new house in memory of his old Peterhead haunts, and the name Mount Pleasant proudly appeared in black lettering on the lintel of the gateway. He lived here for the next quarter of a century and after his death his family leased the house to various tenants. But in 1859 the then owner, Dr Thomas Smith, sold the house to a mason, Charles Stewart, and to the description 'along the bank of the Aberdeenshire Canal' was added 'now along the line of the Great North of Scotland Railway'. Given the spacious feu, one is not surprised to learn that Stewart built a tenement next to Mount Pleasant. That latter property, now tenemented itself, was bought in 1878 by Matthew Croall, a well-known Gallowgate baker. A fellow resident of Mr Croall's at Mount Pleasant, Mr A Gemmel was a stereotyper at the *Aberdeen Journal*, while living in the new tenement next door was another baker, James Gray. The street would attract an interesting variety of residents over the years including a tea merchant, a teacher, a surgeon, a minister, an iron founder, a plumber, a plasterer, a book-keeper and a beadle.

In 1809 King's College feued the site adjoining Mount Pleasant to Alexander Leith. The feudal superior could effectively control the way in which an area would develop by laying down restrictions in the feu charter, and the masters of King's decreed that within three years Leith must erect a building to the value of £60 in stone or brick which had to be tiled or slated. He also had to keep Canal Street - now named as such in the feu charter- 'free from all Obstructions, Dunghills and other Nuisances' while adjoining feuars were obliged 'to bind upon' Leith's house, and maintain them in the same line. One amenity which the Canal Street houses would enjoy was the length of the frontage granted in the charters, usually over 100 feet, which provided ample space in those early days, for elegant gardens and imposing carriage drives.

Leith was a quarrier, and when the purchaser of a new site is so designated, one presumes, as with 'mason', the arrival of the speculative builder; such seems to have been the case with Leith. By 1810 he had sold his new house, No 2 Canal Street, to John Sim, a Spital shoemaker for £53. Prices rose during the century, but with a little 'yo-yoing'. John Smith, the parochial schoolmaster of Peterculter, bought the house for £341 in 1848, while in 1862 it was rouped to Isaac Forsyth, a letter carrier, for only £330. This seems a substantial outlay, but then Forsyth was no ordinary postie. He was one of the pioneering directors of the Northern Co-operative Company, as the Society then was, a regular attender at the fortnightly directors' meetings, often taking the chair. He was much involved in the purchase of the Berryden site in 1878, and when he died two years later there was a 'strong expression of regret' from his fellow directors. His family were equally eident. His daughter taught music and his wife took in lodgers, which she continued to do after his death.

The Aberdeen merchant, James Mellis, was another early resident of Canal Street. His house became the future No 5 for his feu was a substantial one, with space for a further two houses to the east, between himself and No 2. In 1831 Mellis sub-feued land to the east of his house to Jonathan Wright, who built what became No 3 Canal Street. The following year Mellis sub-feued more land between his own dwelling and Wright's to Peter Buchan, the Peterhead printer and ballad collector. The Canalside may have been recommended to Buchan by his fellow blue-mogganer, John Smith of

Mount Pleasant. If this was the case, the fact that Smith died in 1832, the year that Buchan took up residence there, was typical of the bad luck that dogged him throughout his life. It was the writer Thomas Carlyle who on seeing a portrait of Peter Buchan, summed him up as 'a lean-visaged, crane-necked, scraggy-bearded human figure, with an air of enthusiasm, simplicity, distraction and ill-luck'.

By the time Buchan came to Aberdeen in 1831, he was something of a celebrity. In 1790, 'Peterhead had the honour of giving me birth', he modestly notes in his *Autobiographical Sketch* of 1839. His attempts to get himself commissioned midshipman had been scuppered by his disapproving parents, so instead he embarked on a literary career, quickly producing a book of verse. Having developed 'a taste for mechanics' in boyhood, he was able to build his own printing presses from bits and pieces. The second, dating from 1819, was built of wood, iron and brass and was worked by treadle. On it that year he printed his *Annals of Peterhead*, engraving the plates as well, and setting the text directly in type as he created it. He then turned publisher and bookseller, and sold all the copies.

He went on to print and publish a vast and diffuse amount of material, from *Rules and Regulations of the Peterhead Savings Bank* to *The Secret History of Macbeth, King of Scotland.* Biographies, histories, pamphlets, and

Peter Buchan,'. . a scraggy-bearded human figure, with an air of enthusiasm, simplicity, distraction and ill-luck.'

tracts poured forth, many of them written by himself. He even began work on a projected *Dictionary of the Scots Language*. But it was as a ballad collector that he was best known, and his great work in this field, *Ancient Ballads and Songs of the North of Scotland*, published in 1828 brought him public acclaim. In 1831 'I removed with part of my caravanserai' - he had a large family - 'to Aberdeen'. Three of his sons were completing courses at Marischal College. Initially, the caravanserai stayed at Charles Court in the Upperkirkgate which was very handy for the College. The apartment may have been too small, or perhaps Buchan felt his status as a public figure demanded a new and stylish residence, hence the move to Mounthooly. At Canal Street he set about building with 'the best materials', the future No 4, a fine three-storey house of twelve apartments which he named Helicon

Hill after the home of the muses in Greek mythology. He straightway got himself into a fankle, however, by allowing Helicon Hill's east gable to encroach on Jonathan Wright's garden. Letters were exchanged and a gentlemanly compromise was arrived at with Wright taking a small piece of Buchan's land in compensation, with the option of training bushes and trees there, providing they caused no damage. Meanwhile Buchan, according to one of his contacts, 'Coppery' David Anderson, an Inverurie coppersmith and poet, had lost no time in holding soirées for the local *literati*.

Rival street directories appeared in Aberdeen for 1835-36 one produced by the Aberdeen Post Office, 'Printed for the Letter Carriers', which noted Buchan's residence as 'Helicon-hill-house'. The opposition, Chalmers Street Directory gave it inaccurately if more plainly as 'Mounthill'. As it transpired, both were out of date, for by May 1833, the year after it was completed, there was offered for sale:

> that new house fourth from Mounthooly Bridge, Canal Street with its large garden facing south, with pure air, in the country but within minutes walk of the centre of Aberdeen. Apply to the proprietor at the house, Peter Buchan.

What had gone wrong? Buchan, ever one to dramatise his lot, explains in his *Autobiographical Sketch:*

> There - when I name it my blood runs cold - in ABERDEEN was I innocently plundered and indirectly robbed of upwards of seven hundred pounds sterling by the most unprincipled of men...in conjunction with the lowest and most detestable of all human beings, the *pettifogging lawyers.* (Capital letters and italics are Buchan's).

It seems that Buchan, whose financial standing was always precarious, had over-reached himself with the building of Helicon Hill at a time when there were many demands on his resources. Apart from having a wife and numerous children to support, he was one of the few collectors who paid his 'sources', the likes of 'Coppery Davie' and 'Blin Jamie' Rankin who provided him with unpublished ballad material. He was declared bankrupt and as well as having to put Helicon Hill on the market, was forced to sell his library of several thousand volumes 'of the most curious and rare works in print'. In his attack on pettifogging lawyers, Buchan singles out for particularly virulent attack '...these vampires, the Nic-hells'. Perhaps it is a coincidence but on the death in 1841, of an Aberdeen lawyer, Lewis Nicoll, it was noted that he possessed 'a fine library of upwards of 5000 volumes'.

But it was, nevertheless, a young lawyer, Alexander Macdonald, who bailed him out. Helicon Hill was still on the market in 1834, reduced to an upset price of £260 for a quick sale. It was advertised again, and eventually

Macdonald bought it before the end of the year for £110, undertaking to discharge a bond of £150 over the property.

Buchan had moved to one of several cottages at the far end of the street, and announced that valid claims against him would be met in full 'at my present residence No 12 Canal Street'. It seems that the family stayed there, perhaps until 1839, in reduced circumstances, but at least Buchan was able to argue that he did not leave 'that purgatorial place' (Aberdeen rather than Canal Street) 'clandestinely nor under the cloud of night'. In spite of his venomous dislike of local lawyers he had nothing but praise for Alexander Macdonald who came to the rescue yet again with a charming testimonial which would stand Buchan in good stead on his travels:

> Having acted as Law Agent for the bearer, Mr Peter Buchan, for the last five years, I have uniformly found him, amidst the many severe losses to which he has been subjected, to be a person of the strictest honour and integrity, anxiously desirous to give every man his own.

After leaving Aberdeen the family was frequently on the move between Scotland, Ireland and England. Buchan died in London in 1854 while attempting to arrange the publication of some of his works. He had arrived just in time to become the victim of a cholera epidemic that had broken out there.

By a curious coincidence it was during the 1830s that these two geniuses, Robert Davidson and Peter Buchan, largely forgotten by all but specialists in their relative fields, lived across from each other, Davidson in Canal Road and Buchan in Canal Street, on opposite banks of the Aberdeenshire Canal. Apart from the fact that both had invented a printing press, no two men could have been less alike in temperament. Davidson, modest, unassuming, declining to patent his inventions; Buchan, sycophantic, vain, paranoid, fighting lawsuits over patents. Davidson's house crammed with watches, clocks, fine swords, china, works of art and musical instruments; across the water, Buchan's most valued possessions sold up to pay his debts. Davidson, with various thriving businesses to fall back on when his inventions were spurned, spending a lifetime in Canal Road within a happy family circle; Buchan, making a precarious living, often on the move, mourning the death of eight of his ten children.

Buchan's career was marred by the scorn of contemporary literary lions such as Thomas Carlyle and Sir Walter Scott. He was accused, not without some truth, of making up ballads himself, or too easily accepting as genuine, doggerel concocted by the likes of 'Blin Jamie' who was well aware that the generous, ingenuous Buchan was easily parted from his siller. To give an illustration, the renowned Aberdeen historians, John Hill Burton and Joseph Robertson, naughtily concocted fragments of a spoof ballad which they called *Chil Ether*, and presented it to the gullible Peter. It was a splendid 'send up' of the old ballad style:

Chil Ether and Lady Maisey
Were baith born at ae birth;
They loved each other tenderlie
'Boon everything on earth.

Who would suspect so reputable a source? Certainly not Buchan who was completely taken in. 'He not only published the ballad as genuine, ' writes G M Fraser, 'but added a note that he had been able to recover the missing stanzas. These he had written himself...' Nevertheless Buchan was in the *avant-garde* of ballad collecting. Gavin Greig and the Rev James B Duncan in the early twentieth century, and Hamish Henderson and the School of Scottish Studies in more modern times have followed in his footsteps. Notwithstanding his *faux pas,* contemporary scholars of the ballad are fully aware of Buchan's genuine pioneering achievements.

Back among the more mundane of Canal Street's early residents, we find James Coutts Jnr at No 6, next door to James Mellis, Robert Small

Nos 6 and 6a Canal Street. The house on the right could almost be mistaken for a country church.

71

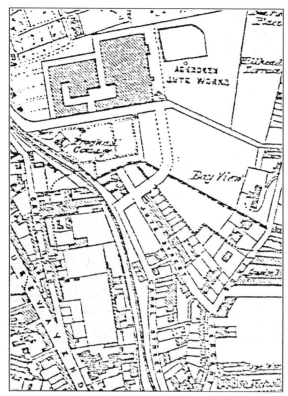

Detail from the Post Office Directory Map of 1880, showing the projected line of Canal Street. It never materialised.

tinsmith, at No 7, and John Clark, flax dresser at No 8. Small's feu charter is dated June 1818, the ground is still part of Humphrie's croft, and the Principal and Professors King's College remain the feudal superiors. Further along was a group of cottages, including No 12 where Buchan finally stayed. Though earlier street directories described Canal Street as running 'from Mounthooly Bridge to Froghall Bridge' the road petered out at No 12, but was continued by a track above the canal, then the railway, to Froghall. The elastic term 'Canalside' was applied to Canal Street, but confusion was usually avoided by adding 'Mounthooly'. Sometime between 1870 and 1880, however, a new scheme was afoot. A pavement was laid out beyond No 12, and Canal Street was then projected to curve north-west to meet Jute Street at its northerly end. This new street would then proceed into the Aberdeen Jute Works as shown above. This plan never came to pass, and the Ordnance Survey of 1901 shows Canal Street turning north where it still does today, meeting Jute Street roughly half way down.

The late Duncan Brand's prize-winning garden at No 7 Canal Street.
Courtesy, Anne Logan.

No 7 had passed to Robert Small's son, William, an ironmonger and by 1877 the owner was John Crichton, a warehouseman which at that time meant a shop owner. A later proprietor was the coal merchant, James Thain, who had his stable and coal yard nearby at Mounthooly, in the Canal Place cul-de-sac. In 1952, the property was acquired by Duncan Brand who until then lived next door at 6a. The purchase price of No 7 was £450 and Mr Brand had a bargain, for James Thain had paid £550 back in 1920, and a later owner, as much as £700. Mr Brand, Head of the Joinery Department at Aberdeen Technical College, later made alterations that provided him with a splendid basement and storage space for his hobbies - and one of these was gardening. No 7 had retained its original long frontage and year after year Duncan Brand was able to create a superb garden, which won him numerous prizes including the local Britain in Bloom in his class.

The two Brand daughters, Anne and Laura had their early schooling nearby at Causewayend Primary and sang with the Aberdeen Arion choir. Later they gained considerable fame, not only in the Aberdeen area but throughout Scotland and beyond, as fine singers whose appearances on stage, radio and television brought pleasure to thousands.

Anne, left, and Laura Brand, a publicity photograph from the 1970s.

Back at Mount Pleasant, Mr George Gordon, a well known member of the Shore Porters Society, had acquired the property in 1946 from the representatives of Matthew Croall the baker. In 1971 his property, along with those of his neighbours, was bought by Aberdeen Corporation who planned to demolish the houses along the line of the street as far as No 5 and replace them with modern flats. It is rather sad to note that in 1971, No 2 for example, was described in Council Minutes as 'vacated slum property'. It seems a pity that those once fine houses, long since converted to tenements, had to be pulled down rather than restored. As it was, demolition did not begin until March 1975, and was eventually concluded in August 1976 and a modern complex of eight three-storey and two four-storey blocks was then built on the Canal Street-King's Crescent corner. Mr Gordon, who has carried out much research on Canal Street and King's Crescent, as well as writing histories of the Shore Porters and of the Gordon family, had the foresight to request the local authority that John Smith's fine granite archway be spared. He writes:

It was, and there it stands today, a fragment of the past, the only reminder that once upon a time it gave entry to a property on the Canalside called Mount Pleasant.

'A fragment of the past', the Mount Pleasant arch. Though not visible in the photograph, the observant passer-by can still decipher the 'P' and 'T' of Pleasant.

Helicon Hill at No 4 was among those taken down, as was Peter Buchan's other, more modest residence at No 12 at the far end. He never had much luck. That latter demolition was part of another housing initiative by Aberdeen Corporation, the end product of which was the creation by 1974 of thirty flats at the junction of Canal Street and Jute Street. The Housing

The last two cottages in Canal Street. The flats to the rear, left, won a Saltire Society Commendation.

75

Committee, under the direction of the city architect T C Watson received a Saltire Society commendation for the scheme. The project architect was Mr Sandy Reith who has since gone on to do much interesting work in the Spital in a private capacity. Canal Street never experienced the industrialisation which came to Canal Road, and which in the end was its undoing. Canal Street remains a pleasant residential row with its original dwellings, a mix of handsome houses and attractive cottages to be found between No 6-11, while two complexes of modern flats stand guard at either end.

Local residents enjoy a sunny afternoon in Canal Street. The modern flats behind are near the old Mount Pleasant site.

Perhaps this might be the place to add a footnote about Friendly Bank, Mount Pleasant's opposite number on the other side of Mounthooly Bridge. The names of both houses provided a cheery-sounding start to the journey to Old Aberdeen; the Pleasant Mount and the Friendly Bank, the bank being that of the canal which flowed along the bottom of the garden - though there was some uncertainty as to this house's true whereabouts. For its first hundred years the address was Friendly Bank, Mounthooly, but early in twentieth century it became No 2 King's Crescent.

For many years it was the home of Samuel Willans, stoneware manufacturer, and very handy too, for his business was based at the old Porthill Factory until the 1860s. Around the turn of the century it was even handier for William Dalgleish , governor of the East (or St Nicholas) Poorhouse,

*Friendly Bank's gateposts
survived until 1994.*

round the corner in Nelson Street. Dalgleish lived virtually over the shop, for the grounds of Friendly Bank and of the Poorhouse adjoined, and a little flight of steps at his back door provided a handy short cut for the governor.

This palatial institution, (the Poorhouse, not Friendly Bank) had opened for business in 1849 and the census returns of 1851 show a curiously mixed bag of about 280 residents which was well under capacity; a beggar, a washerwoman, servants, a stocking knitter, a nailer's wife, a deserted wife, scholars, a farm servant. Many were incomers - from Edinburgh, the Highlands, Bishop Auckland; a hawker from Fife, a weaver's pirner from Orkney, four children by the name of Hoby from Stockton, a labourer's wife from Ceylon; Thomas Ryder, comedian, (an actor) was a boarder, a distinction carefully made. Joseph Colstaff, a street musician came from Genoa, Italy. Perhaps they had sing-songs of an evening.

The Poorhouse was taken down early in the twentieth century, and Alex Slessor can remember, as a child, seeing the piles of stones which were left on the site for years. In 1937 St Peter's R C Primary School was built here and susequently suffered from subsidence, possibly caused by the old 'bulges' of the canal. St Peter's flitted to King Street in 1983, and a police establishment, its foundations deeply excavated, has replaced the school.

Returning to Friendly Bank, George Gordon recalls that during the small-pox epidemic of the 1870s the house, for long a doctor's residence and surgery, was used as an auxiliary hospital. By 1910 it had become a Church of Scotland Hone for Boys. Friendly Bank lay derelict for many years, and in 1977 suffered the same fate as Mount Pleasant.

Part Three

Churches and Schools

The Tower, Causewayend School

Powis Church
from the original watercolour by J A Sutherland.
The illustration on page 23 shows the same site prior to 1894.

Chapter 7

'And still there came more Churches...'

Controversial talks on the closure of a historic Aberdeen Church (St Stephen's) collapsed late last night amid a bitter debate.

Press & Journal, September 6, 1995

As the nineteenth century wore on, the arrival of many working class families in the new streets between Mounthooly and George Street had not gone unnoticed by the ministers of the Aberdeen Presbytery. Their first attempt to reach out to the souls there was rather curious, but no doubt seemed a good idea at the time. Chapels of Ease had earlier been set up around the outskirts of the city, at Gilcomston and Woodside for example, to provide an easier means of worship for those who lived far from their parish church. A Gaelic Chapel, established in 1795, was rather different. It served no embryonic parish, but Highland incomers in general. In 1834 after the Chapel Act upgraded such chapels to parish church status, (though *quoad sacra* parishes, that is, for religious purposes only) it occurred to the Presbytery that the Gaelic Chapel could now be regarded as a parish church although it had no parish, while the Mounthooly-George Street area, centring around Spring Garden, was an embryonic parish without a church. Why not unite the two? And so the Gaelic Chapel, doubtless to the surprise of its congregation, was renamed Spring Garden (Gaelic) Parish Church, in spite of being located in the heart of the city, in Gaelic Lane. For their part, the new parishioners, most of them Doric speakers, must have

A rare photograph of the first John Knox's Church, (1835-1910) facing out across Mounthooly. Courtesy, John Knox's Church.

been puzzled to find themselves attached to a distant church where worship was conducted in Gaelic, a language they did not understand. In the years to come, it was the ministers who preached in the Doric who would draw the greatest crowds in and around Mounthooly.

Spring Garden Parish appears to have been a dead duck from the start, but in any case, the man virtually on the spot, the charismatic Reverend Abercromby Gordon of Greyfriars Parish Church in Broad Street, had better ideas. 'He was,' Alexander Gammie the church historian tells us, 'a man of rare powers, of lofty character, zealous for the interests of the church.' Greyfriars had become one of the six new civic parishes in 1828, and Abercromby Gordon now pressed for a new extension church for 'the populous district of Causewayend, Hutcheon Street etc.' the northern outpost of his parish. He went proselytising down the Gallowgate, and by September 1834, £380 of the necessary £550 had been raised towards a church with seating for over 500. The walls would be high enough to incorporate galleries at a later date, giving a capacity of around 1000. It was decided to go ahead as soon as the additional £170 was raised for 'this cheap, and most necessary and useful work.' In fact the gun was jumped. Three weeks later and with only £10 knocked off the deficit, the Greyfriars Parish Association was advertising for 'contractors to build and finish a Church at

Mounthooly'. In October, the foundation stone was laid and the new kirk, plain but imposing, opened for worship a few months later in May 1835, with every inch of sitting and standing room taken up long before the hour of worship. And rather unusually for a nineteenth century church, a burial ground was attached, wedge-shaped and running as far back as the Canal. No reason was given for the choice of name. In the sixteenth century, Aberdeen had participated in the Reformation strictly on its own terms and John Knox, who had visited the city but once, was not a local hero.

Churches of all denominations at that time played a major role in educating working class children in Scotland, and Abercromby Gordon, the force behind the establishment of the Porthill Schools in the Gallowgate, envisaged that a school 'for which there is a great necessity' would be attached to the new kirk from the outset. A school with adjoining rooms, one for boys and one for girls and infants was built between church and churchyard and an evening school for factory girls in Chronicle Lane between West North Street and Mealmarket Street, now relocated there.

Not a decade had passed after the building of John Knox's Kirk when the Disruption broke upon the Church of Scotland. The argument was over the right of the laird or patron of the church in question to appoint a minister even though the congregation might find such an appointment 'obnoxious'. This was unacceptable to many worshippers and at the General Assembly in Edinburgh in May 1843 over a third of the ministers left the Church of Scotland or 'came out' - the phrase had a rather different meaning in those days - many bringing their entire congregation with them. Thus was the Free Kirk established. In Aberdeen the Town Council was patron of the parish churches, and it was not the magistrates' policy to 'intrude' ministers against the wishes of the congregation. Nevertheless the ministers of all the city parishes came out in support of the Free Kirk movement.

A bloodless battle ensued at John Knox's when the minister, John Stephen, a Fittie man, and the bulk of his congregation, around 1100, threw in their lot with the Free Kirk. Their tactics were to 'come out' by staying put, arguing that John Knox's was on a different and lesser footing than the city kirks which were *quoad civilia* par-ish churches, serving fully fledged

Old Free John Knox Church,
Gerrard Street.

83

civic parishes. The Presbytery had no intention of accepting this distinction and a petition claiming the kirk and school buildings on behalf of the Free Kirk, signed by well over 1000 people, cut no ice. The minister and his followers had to leave. After Stephen's last service:

> the scene in the street outside was memorable. The people remained in a body outside the building until they saw it left for the last time by their minister, who was saluted with melancholy and respectful solemnity as he passed through the crowd on his way home.

The rump of sixty adherents of the Auld Kirk, as the Established Church of Scotland was now known, was ministered to by the Reverend Charles Skene, former dominie of Skene parish school and damned with faint praise by Alexander Gammie as 'an earnest kindly faithful man who laboured in the charge with conscientious diligence though with no outstanding success'. His successor, the Reverend Herbert Bell met with a fatal accident at Kittybrewster Station in 1887, but that tragedy occurred after a stimulating ministry of ten years during which membership soared again. John Knox's was disjoined from the mother church of Greyfriars to become a parish church in its own right in 1880, and a hall was built to cope with the steadily expanding Sunday School.

The Rev George A Johnston.

The ministry of the Reverend George A Johnston lasted only three years, from 1906 until 1909, but was so memorable that older members of the congregation recall that his name was a household word in their childhood. There had been something of a *contretemps* at his previous incumbency and Johnston went freelance for a time. But he had the reputation of being a considerable preacher and though the Poor Law Amendment Act of 1846 had relieved the Kirk of the obligation to provide for the poor, large congregations and the ensuing bulging collection bags were still essential for the well-being of each church and the agencies it supported. Hence the need to call a minister who was a crowd-puller and John Knox's was determined to have George A Johnston. The call, however, had to be put on 'hold' for a time while his position was thrashed out by the Aberdeen Presbytery and then by the

John Knox's Mounthooly.

General Assembly. Johnston, eventually inducted, went on to attract great crowds by his vigorous preaching, often in the Doric. With a congregation now numbering well over 2000, the church was filled to overflowing. A bigger and better church on the same site was the obvious solution.

Fund-raising, organised by Johnston's successor, the Reverend A M Snadden, included the fashionable method of the three day bazaar which was held in 1910 at the Music Hall. The following year the foundation stone of John Knox's II was laid by Mrs W H Coats, the future Lady Glentanar, wife of the Paisley thread tycoon, so we can assume that this open-handed family were major benefactors.

The architects were Wilsons and Walker. Wilson *père* had an excellent pedigree as an ecclesiastical architect, having been the apprentice, and subsequently the partner of Alexander 'Holy' Ellis, by then in retirement, but renowned for his work at St Mary's Episcopal Church, Carden Place, and St Mary's Roman Catholic Cathedral, Huntly Street. The impressive John Knox's Church, its handsome entrance flanked by columns, is reminiscent of a Roman temple. At first floor level there is a balcony with three windows and above, an open pediment with balustrades at the corners. The halls are below, rather in the style of an undercroft, making skilful use of varying levels, with a beadle's house to the rear. The earlier kirk had looked west across the narrow street of Mounthooly, but the architects now boldly turned the frontage of the new building 45° southwards to dominate the crossroads.

Returning to the stirring days of the Disruption, we had left the Reverend John Stephen and his John Knox Free Kirkers without a church. The week after the eviction from Mounthooly, over 1000 of Stephen's followers gathered amid scenes of great enthusiasm at Routledge and Sons' Rope Works in Catherine Street. They decided there and then to build a new church nearby in Gerrard Street where a site was available. Schooling would continue to be given a high priority. Eight months later, the new kirk, 'plain but substantial', with boys' and girls' schools on the east and west sides respectively was ready, with seating for 1200.

The Rev Robert Macleod.

John Knox Free, or United Free (UF) as it became in 1900 after the union of the Free and United Presbyterian Churches, continued with great success in its catchment area which was becoming increasingly industrialised and heavily populated. Much of its popularity was due to John Stephen's strong personality. He had been a student of the legendary Dr Kidd of Gilcomston, one of the greatest preachers Aberdeen had known, and whose funeral in December 1834 had brought the city to a standstill. One of Stephen's most outstanding successors, called in 1883, was the Reverend Robert Macleod who had taught at the well known Old Aberdeen boys' school, the Gymnasium, while studying Divinity. Although 'the westward tendency in the city' as Gammie calls it was well underway by then, membership nevertheless increased during MacLeod's ministry, and the kirk was particularly popular with young folk.

A new church became a priority. As a preliminary step, the girls' school was demolished and the fine new hall which replaced it was used for worship until the new kirk, built on the same site, was complete. This handsome building contrasted spectacularly with the poorer tenements of Gerrard Street. It opened for worship in 1900. There were seats for 918 and the cost was £6000. Unlike some free kirks of this era, it has no soaring spire and cannot be seen from afar, though for a few months in 1993 it gave the impression of arising miraculously from the debris of the old Mckinnon's Iron Works. One must get close to appreciate its bold detail. Italiante in style, the frontage is dominated by chamfered or 'grooved' masonry and by

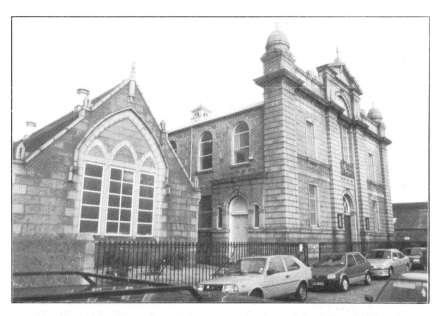

The former John Knox, Gerrard Street, now the Gerrard Street Baptist Church.

four pilasters or columns. Those on the corners are topped by small square towers and cupolas, while the central pair flank a handsome doorway and fanlight. The latter bears a unique feature, a keystone Knox, a small but beautiful head of the great reformer carved in granite. Above two of the upper windows are inscribed the dates AD 1843 and AD 1898 indicating respectively the original Disruption kirk, and the foundation of the present building. The architect was George Coutts whose office was nearby in John Street. Around this time he also designed the splendid, soaring 'Star and Garter' block near the top of Crown Street and a little later, the handsome No 1 Rubislaw Den North in pink and grey granite with towering Tudor-style gables.

As it happens, 1898, the year of the foundation of the Gerrard Street kirk was also the year that the Palace Theatre in Bridge Place was rebuilt after a horrendous fire. The two buildings are not unlike - the original plans for the rebuilt Palace even included cupolas. Bon-Accord Congregational Church in Bon-Accord Terrace, subsequently the Buffaloes' Institute and now the local British Legion headquarters, also belongs to this era in local architecture when the designs of churches and theatres seemed inter-changeable. Indeed it would not be many years before a number of churches were converted, quite easily, into picture-houses.

The former Bon-Accord Congregational Church.

'The designs of churches and theatres seemed interchangeable'. Above, plans for the Palace, Bridge Place, show similarities with the former John Knox, Gerrard Street and with the former Bon Accord Congregational Church, now the headquarters of the British Legion, Aberdeen.

The John Knox Free complex in Gerrard Street was completed by a rubble-built mission hall on the east side and a Sunday School to the rear. In 1929, after the union of the Established and United Free Kirks, the Auld Kirk became, John Knox's, Mounthooly, and the Free Kirk, John Knox, Gerrard Street. The latter kirk during this period had an outstanding minister in the Reverend Alexander Frazer, a great evangelist who held open air meetings in the Castlegate. His fame spread far beyond Aberdeen and during 1931 he preached throughout much of the Commonwealth. The Reverend Laurie Y Gordon, minister at Mounthooly, tells me that his own kirk was always known as 'John Knox's', and the Gerrard Street church as 'John Knox'.

If the two John Knoxes were the most prominent kirks in the area, they were by no means the only ones. In 1867 a new church, the Nelson Street United Presbyterian, (the UPs were an amalgamation of pre-Disruption secessionists) appeared a few yards across from John Knox's, Mounthooly. It did not enjoy the success of its neighbourhood rivals and in 1909 amalgamated with St Andrew's UF on the King Street-Urquhart Road corner to form King Street UF. This building later became home to the Assemblies of God. By 1912 the former Nelson Street UP building had gone

Now refurbished as offices and a golf centre, the former Nelson Street UP Church, alias the 'Globie' retains its bulky ecclesiastical outlines.

from salvation to damnation, reincarnated as the Globe Picture Playhouse. The 'Globie', still remembered with affection by its former clientele, closed in 1940, re-opening that same year as a forces' training centre. These days, after more recent refurbishments, the 'Globie' continues as a golf centre and offices. But the ecclesiastical outlines of the old Nelson Street UP are clearly to be seen behind the smart façade.

The Salvation Army's first custom-built hall in Aberdeen was in Windy Wynd, and they also had a 'slum post' in West North Street, where the Wesleyan Methodists were also to be found for a time. Most churches ran their own missions but in 1874, following the visit of Moody and Sankey to Aberdeen, a mission started in a Charles Street tenement, to minister to the folk of the densely populated alleyways between the Causewayend Road and North Broadford, the upper part of George Street. Subsequently, under the auspices of the YMCA, it flourished for many years as the Causewayend Mission, latterly with Miss Elizabeth Copland in charge. It closed in 1974 and was subsequently demolished to make way for the new dual carriageway.

And still there came more churches. In 1871 the city boundary which previously ran between Hutcheon Street and Charles Street was extended out to North Broadford and Kittybrewster. The prominent free churchman, Sir William Henderson, calculated that in the area between Mounthooly and Kittybrewster there were 1209 families, roughly 5300 souls, within the city boundary and many more just outside the boundary. In spite of the success of the Causewayend Mission, he felt that nothing less than a fully fledged kirk with its attendant Sunday School, Band of Hope and Bible Woman would do to serve the Hutcheon Street-Kittybrewster wedge. Gammie hints at some opposition but Sir William was not

Sir William Henderson, Lord Provost of Aberdeen from 1886-1888,'was not so much a pillar of the Free Kirk as a veritable edifice...'

one to be easily deflected. He was a highly successful businessman, a partner with his father-in-law, Provost George Thomson, in the world-famous shipping company, the Aberdeen White Star Line. (Thomson himself was a son-in-law of none other than the formidable Dr Kidd of Gilcomston). Sir William was not so much a pillar of the Free Kirk as a veritable edifice, pouring his profits into the building of several fine kirks then being established in the city as part of the Free Church extension movement.

In the spring of 1877 Henderson and his Free Kirk colleagues reconnoitred the Causewayend Road, North Broadford and Kittybrewster. They had their eye on Split-the Wind, but ruled it out. Even if the site were available, its commanding position would, they felt, have called for ornate - and expensive - frontages to North Broadford and Powis Place. Moreover it was too far out. They eventually decided on a site where a gardener, James Berry, once had a steading and market garden. He had given his name to the area though this Berry Street was not to be confused with Berry Street off the Gallowgate. In fact it was none other than 'the litill cassy,' of ancient memory, once a 'gate' of some importance. When James Berry worked there during the mid-nineteenth century it was called Broadford Lane, but readers will know it best as Powis Lane. One suspects the hand of the Leslies when that change came about. The lane linked both forks of

Powis Lane, the link that gave access to Causewayend Kirk.

*St Stephen's Church, Powis Terrace was built in 1879
as Causewayend Free Church.*

the turnpike, and Henderson and his colleagues could be sure of attracting numerous members from North Broadford as well as the Causewayend Road and Canal Road areas. And so Causewayend Free Church was built fronting Causewayend or, to be completely accurate, the newly created Powis Place.

The architect Duncan McMillan who worked closely with Henderson, produced designs for a church that was not unlike, though more graceful than the earlier Holburn Parish (now Holburn Central) with a classical frontage and a tower, supporting a miniature 'bandstand' of eight Tuscan columns and a dome, capped by a weather vane. The new kirk, built at a cost of over £1000 and paid for by Sir William Henderson, opened in 1879. A number of embellishments were added during the ministry of the Reverend James A Russell from 1886 until 1918. A chiming clock, known locally as the Powis Clock was installed on the tower in 1896 - the Town subsequently took over its maintenance - followed by side galleries, tinted glass and an organ.

Isaac Benzie, the hosier, had joined the congregation in 1903 when he was living nearby in Clifton Road. A faithful member of the kirk all his life, he remained an elder and a superintendent of one of Causewayend's two flourishing Sunday Schools for eight years in spite of the pressures of building up a new department store, one of the finest in the city. His eldest son, Mr Isaac, a talented pianist and organist died at the early age of 42 in 1935. Like his father he was a devoted member of Cassie-end, and just before he was taken ill on the afternoon of Christmas Day, he had brought along his cinematograph to the church hall and treated the congregation to a film show.

Isaac Benzie's involvement is interesting for the congregations under discussion were, as Gammie stressed in *The Churches of Aberdeen* (1909), almost entirely working class. If one was not working class, one apparently went elsewhere. Robert Davidson, the Canal Road electrical genius, and John Sutherland, who built Viewton Place in King's Crescent, both lived a stone's throw from John Knox's. Yet Davidson went to the West Church and Sutherland was an Auld Licht Anti-Burger. But fashions had changed and by the 1920s, a good preacher drew crowds from far and near. Writing in *Life and Work* in October 1966, the playwright, Robert Kemp, remembered that:

My grandmother, with whom I went to stay while I attended school in Aberdeen was a member of John Knox's Church in Mounthooly. It was perhaps not the nearest church - I seem to recall that we always left home at twenty minutes to the hour in order to be in time for the service - but it housed a large congregation, spellbound in those days by the eloquent preaching of the Reverend D Finlay Clarke.

In his article Kemp went on to recall happy memories of the John Knox's Boys' Brigade, especially playing for the football team. 'The old BB uniform was worn with pride as we strode in company under the gas lamps of Causewayend to the hall below the kirk .'

A church was eventually built at Split-the-Wind. The Kittybrewster district by the late nineteenth century had an estimated population of 5000, and the fact that the only church in the area was the popular Causewayend Free was a sore point with the Auld Kirk. As Gammie put it tactfully: 'It was felt that the Established Church, in justice to its traditions, had a duty to perform for its members in the district'. The Split-the-Wind site, part of the Lands of Calsayseat, was owned by the Misses Leslie of Powis who in 1888 gifted it to the Church of Scotland as noted in Chapter Two. The sisters had, a decade earlier, sold a portion of their estate to allow the expansion of the railway complex at Kittybrewster. Although handsomely rewarded, they were nevertheless dismayed by resulting loss of amenity at Powis House.

John Knox's, Mounthooly, founded the 37th Aberdeen Company of the Boy's Brigade in 1926. This picture shows a reunion of officers, leaders, juniors and 'old boys' marking the 50th anniversary in December, 1976. The minister of John Knox's, the Rev Laurie Gordon is seated in the centre of the third row.

The three surviving elderly ladies now stipulated that the new kirk should be known as Powis Church, even though it was at the very threshold of Kittybrewster. Thus, yet again, they commemorated their beloved estate and banished the stressful name of Kittybrewster.

Funds for the new kirk were raised under the auspices of the Aberdeen Church Extension Scheme and by 1894 it was felt that there was enough money in the kitty to proceed. The House of Calsay Seat and the former 'Coffin' were demolished. The architect, A Marshall Mackenzie, who had done excellent work in George Street had produced plans. Apparently unmindful of the fact that the maintenance of the church would fall to a largely working class congregation, he let his enthusiasm for the prominence of the site go to his head, indulging himself in a cathedralesque structure with a 'lofty and graceful spire', a nave and transepts. The axis wasn't quite right for a choir. Although Powis Church was to begin life as a humble Chapel of Ease in the parish of Oldmachar it seems that Marshall Mackenzie was attempting to emulate the mother church, St Machar's Cathedral itself. Fortunately lack of funds and common sense prevailed and the church which eventually appeared in 1895 'at Calsay Seat' to give Split-the-Wind its official name, at a cost of £2500, was Mackenzie's elegant nave alone.

'The church that never was'
The original design for Powis Church
exploited the prominent site but was
financially impracticable.

Back at Causewayend, Russell had been succeeded by the Reverend Dr W D Niven, one of Scotland's most distinguished ecclesiastical scholars and later Professor of Church History at Glasgow University. Dr Niven, minister from 1919 until 1927, was virtually contemporary with Finlay Clarke at John Knox's. A major scheme of reconstruction and redecoration got underway to mark Cassie-end's 50th jubilee, and was completed by 1932 under Dr Niven's successor, the Reverend William McNaught. During these inter-war years, Cassie-end Sunday School picnics were held in the grounds of Powis House and are still well-remembered by those who took part.

Disaster struck during the air raid of April 21, 1943 when the kirk took a direct hit. A bomb fell on the doorstep and the front of the church collapsed. For a time worship was shared with the congregation at Powis Church up the road, but within months the hall was patched up and services resumed there for the duration. The church itself was rebuilt after the war and the clock on the tower started chiming the hours again. The side galleries were not rebuilt. The movement of population away from the area was evident by that time. The cost was just under £17000, largely funded by the War Damage Commission though the congregation raised over £3000. Professor Niven preached at the service of rededication in April 1951.

John Knox, Gerrard Street, also suffered slight bomb damage during this raid. After the war, John Knox, had, from 1952-69, an outstanding minister in the Reverend John Birbeck MC, a former chaplain to the Scottish Commandos, and after the war, peripatetic Presbyterian minister to the Middle East where he established eleven centres of Christian worship. One of the high points of his ministry was the setting up of Friendship House, largely through the labours of the congregation, in one of the disused halls where old folk could go for companionship, warmth, a meal, even a bath. This facility was much appreciated, for in the mid-1950s, there were a number of elderly people in the area still living in condemned property, perhaps alone.

The post-war period had brought a number of problems for the

The Rev John Birbeck.

Not the head of John the Baptist, but 'a small but beautiful head of John Knox' above the fanlight of Gerrard Street Church.

churches. The demolition of so many old tenements in the area and the resettling of the population in the new council estates naturally affected congregation numbers. At Mounthooly, the Reverend Laurie Gordon, inducted in 1968, has, since 1987, ministered to the flock of a united John Knox. The Gerrard Street Kirk had lacked a permanent minister since 1985 and amalgamation had been under discussion for some time. Church of Scotland arbiters decreed that the Mounthooly building be the chosen place of worship, to the inevitable disappointment, indeed bitterness, of some of the Gerrard Street congregation, who were, nevertheless, returning to the original fold. As it happened, the congregation of Gilcomston Park Baptist Church were looking for larger premises at this time and decided to take over the Gerrard Street building which is now home to the thriving Gerrard Street Baptist Church.

In 1988 Causewayend Kirk amalgamated with its neighbour, Powis Church at Split-the-Wind. Causewayend became the chosen place of worship, changing its name to St Stephen's Church, though for many it will always be Cassie-end Kirk. The Powis Church building began a secular career by housing a furniture showroom, and subsequently, at time of writing an office equipment centre. St Mary's Episcopal Church, Carden Place provided a home for the Powis organ, built by the master craftsman,

E H Lawton, in 1901.

In October 1988, Aberdeen Presbytery, in the course of a wide-ranging survey of city kirks, recommended that the Mounthooly-Powis area would be best served by one strong church, but stressed that the congregations of John Knox and St Stephen's first be given time to consolidate their recent unions. A wise decision for the union of two kirks is a difficult and sensitive time for both congregations. Further amalgamations seemed inevitable, however, and in September,1995, proposals to unite John Knox's and St Stephen's, with John Knox's becoming the chosen place of worship met with bitter opposition from members of the St Stephen's congregation.

Chapter 8

Schools: Cassie-end and the Middle

At the passing of the Scotch Education Act in 1872, some 3000 children in Aberdeen were destitute of the opportunity, even if they had desired it, of frequenting school...

Thomas Hector, Clerk to Aberdeen School Board, 1907

In 1872 the Education (Scotland) Act made education compulsory (though not yet free), for five to thirteen year-olds, and the responsibility of School Boards. The following year the newly elected Aberdeen School Board took over from the kirk sessions and the trustees of endowed schools who until then had provided much of the education in the city. The Board's ultimate aim, however, was to establish its own schools and quickly identified five densely-populated areas in the city where the need was urgent. One such area was the triangle formed by Causewayend, Hutcheon Street and North Broadford, and accordingly, the building of a new school at Causewayend went ahead during 1875-76.

This was the Board's second custom-built public school, Commerce Street being the first, and it was as grand as the others of that era. It cost a pricey £8657, but the explanation was that: 'contracts had to be entered on at a period of exceptional activity in the building trade and of consequent high prices both for labour and materials'. The designs were by the architect of Balmoral Castle, William Smith, son of John and his successor as city architect. This explains the school's most distinctive feature, a plainer version of the Balmoral tower at the north end. It offered no classroom

William Smith, the architect of Causewayend.

space, but in later years was used to store 'dummies' for the sewing class, stage props and the like

The opening ceremony on February 1, 1877, in the presence of 'a large assemblage' of the great and the good was carried out by a Board member, John Black. 'Large and cumbrous, with a kindly heart and much humanity in his unwieldy frame', Black, a former school inspector, was, by then was Professor of Humanity (Latin) at Aberdeen University. Staff numbered twenty-two including thirteen pupil-teachers, some of whom, in those pre-training college days, would complete their studies at Aberdeen and Edinburgh Universities. The usual public school format of infant, junior and senior departments was in operation and in addition to the basic subjects there was instruction in French and Latin grammar for the older pupils who were, reported an early inspector, 'taught with great vigour'. This style of teaching had mixed results. In 1878 three boys did well enough to go on to Gordon's Hospital (the name was changed to Gordon's College three years later) while Alexander Beaton was expelled for refusing to take the belt, a remarkable rebellion given the awe, if not the fear in which authority was held at that time. Most of the children, however were 'extremely well-behaved and do what they are told very readily'.

Window detail from the original block of Causewayend School, immediately right of the tower.

High days and holidays occasionally interrupted the routine, following the same pattern as at other Aberdeen Board schools. There were holidays for Fast Days which had long lost their religious significance, for the Timmer Market, the Aberdeen Races, and several circuses. A day off, removal day, was generally allowed at term, a city as well as a country practice, when numerous families flitted either in search of better or cheaper accommodation or so that the menfolk could be nearer their work. There were two consecutive days' holiday in 1883, one for the bazaar to raise funds for the new Sick Children's' Hospital in Castle Terrace, the other for the opening of the Duthie Park by Queen Victoria's daughter, Princess Beatrice. A penny savings bank was instituted and there were regular visits from ministers and educationists, one of the most conscientious being Dr William Milligan, Professor of Biblical Criticism, the father of Mrs Katherine Trail, who later wrote such memorable period pieces on Old Aberdeen. On the occasion of Queen Victoria's Golden Jubilee in 1887 our old friend Sir William Henderson, by now Lord Provost, came to distribute medals. A later visitor was School Board member Alexander Inkson McConnochie, climber, hill walker, author of the well known guidebooks, *Deeside*, *Donside*, and *Bennachie*, and secretary of the Aberdeen Fresh Air Fortnight Scheme for Poor Children, which was enjoyed by many young Cassie-enders.

Of fresh air there was much need. Even by the end of the first year, the school, built to accommodate 700, was, coping with over 1000 scholars. In 1889, just over a decade later, there was a new note in HM Inspector's Annual Report. Teaching standards were praised as usual, but the school itself was condemned as 'badly appointed', work being carried on under great difficulties with insufficient and unsuitable accommodation. Ventilation was bad, 'especially in the sewing room, where the atmosphere is poisonous'.

The Board called in the original firm of architects to make improvements. Its *persona* had changed. William Smith was on his deathbed, and William Kelly, his apprentice back in 1877, and who would become one of the city's great architects, was now at the helm. Some internal structural changes were made during the ensuing year providing 'additional comfort', but the two large infant rooms were still overcrowded and infants were being turned away by the hundred.

At this time, 1890, there was an interesting diversion. The School Board found itself examining the Causewayend School tower as a suitable resting place for the superannuated Town House Clock, graciously gifted to them by Aberdeen Corporation. A public clock would be an asset in an area where the ownership of timepieces, bar Robert Davidson's collection, was doubtless a rarity. The Board, however, discovered that the tower would have to be heightened if the clock were to be widely visible, while repairs to the mechanism would cost almost as much as a new one. Carefully looking their gift horse in the mouth, the Board decided they had more urgent uses for their funds, such as an extension to the school. Causewayend Free Church came to the rescue, installing a chiming clock a few years later as already noted.

The solution to the overcrowding lay in the demolition and remodelling of the rear of the school, and expansion to the south. There were also plans to add a gym and cookery block. Such drastic measures would entail closure for over a year but alternative accommodation had first to be found for 1000 scholars. The completion of a new school at Skene Square now brought some relief. Dr Brown's, the original school in that area, had been transferred to the Board in 1879 and according to their usual practice, a bigger and better replacement, Skene Square Public School, or at least its original block had been built. The dominie at Dr Brown's, the kindly and brilliant John Roy LLD, was retiring, and the headmaster of Causewayend now became the first headmaster of Skene Square. In September 1892, hundreds of little Cassie-enders would have been seen straggling along Maberly Street towards their new, if temporary, school.

The Board also found it necessary to rent the 'recently completed and extensive Sunday School buildings at Porthill' and kit them out 'to serve as a gathering place until the opening of the enlarged erection at Causewayend'. With places for 1000 young folk, Porthill was the largest Sunday School in the city, and was also a centre for evening classes and clubs.

The story of its founder, Archibald Reith, is an interesting one. In 1864, this twenty-seven-year-old doctor, regarded as one who would go far in his profession, was appointed junior physician to the Royal Infirmary. He was an enthusiastic pioneer of homeopathy, the curing of like with like, much to the disapproval of his seniors who engaged him in a fierce controversy when they discovered he was treating his patients at Woolmanhill with homeopathic medicines. The row resounded not only in Aberdeen but throughout the medical world. Eventually the senior physicians

Dr Archibald Reith.

threatened mass resignation were Reith, who was due for re-election to the post in 1869, re-appointed. His 'stirring up' of the medical profession was not appreciated by the hospital managers, who declined to re-elect him to the Royal Infirmary. Reith devoted the rest of his life both to his private practice and to his charitable work. As medical officer to the city's General Dispensary, he had the insanitary slums of the Gallowgate as his district.

The memorial to Dr Reith.

Here he discovered that the extant Porthill Sunday School was in a poor way and took it under his wing, devoting over thirty years of his life to the welfare of its scholars. It was thanks to his exertions that a new building was completed immediately south of the former Porthill Factory, just across the Seamount Place divide. At a cost of £7000, this temporary headquarters for some of the Cassie-end pupils had been almost as expensive to build as their own school. Today a granite memorial outside Porthill Court, dedicated to Dr Reith, marks the site of the Porthill Sunday Schools.

Back at Causewayend, things did not go according to plan. When the children moved into the 'enlarged erection' at the beginning of 1894, it was in a dangerously unfinished state with a joiners' strike underway, no handrails on the stairs, no gas supply connected and a lack of glass partitions between classes. Some of those in place were faulty and one fell out, cutting a teacher's face. The school then had to be closed again 'to allow tradesmen to alter the sliding partitions'. By April however, all was complete, and Cassie-end could now cope with 1350 pupils. Teachers busied themselves hanging maps and pictures for an Open Day, and a photograph from this era shows handsome iron railings outside the school, gate piers of granite , a row of trees in the playground and girls in smart white pinafores outside. Such was Kelly's skill that the original school and

Causewayend School after its extension at the end of the nineteenth century. Permission, City of Aberdeen - Arts and Recreation Division - Library Services.

its extension form a seamless whole. One has only to look at the later extensions tagged on to fine schools such as Ruthrieston to appreciate how standards in school architecture have declined, with rising costs no doubt the culprit.

Seniors were now being 'streamed' into two classes, 'the one containing the brightest pupils, the other the more backward'. No mincing of words in those days. But H M Inspector gave 'unstinted praise,' to the standard of teaching of the latter class, adding, 'It is difficult to see where it could be improved.' But in spite of the enlargement of the school, the spectre of overcrowding soon returned. By 1903 the roll had reached 1500 and children were having to sit on window sills. The church halls of Causewayend UF and both John Knoxes had to be pressed into service. However the opening of St Paul Street School in 1897 and the magnificent Kittybrewster School soon after relieved some of the pressure as Cassie-end scholars living at the northern and southern edges of the catchment area were deployed to these new schools.

During the First World War, work proceeded as normal apart from the suspension of cookery lessons to allow the teaching of 'War Economy Cooking' to local women. One of the teachers at this time, the only woman graduate then on the staff was Miss Williamina Williamson. (In 1917 she moved to the High School for Girls where she remained until her retirement in the early 1950s. Many former pupils will recall her as the larger-than-life, dedicated head of 'No 18').

During the great flu epidemics of 1918, and 1919 Cassie-end closed for a month at a time, and throughout the 1920s there were frequent outbreaks of measles, whooping cough and scarlet fever, not helped any by continuing overcrowding though the erection of temporary buildings gave some respite. Attendance dropped regularly in cold and wet weather because of 'bad boots' which are noted regularly in the school log and the teachers themselves were often absent through illness. Up the road in the Gallowgate, the Middle School which opened the same year as Causewayend, was at the centre of a notorious incident in which some Cassie-enders were involved. Two girls there were discovered to have nits in their long hair. The school medical officer, Dr Rose (whose daughter Beatrice later became a formidable headmistress of the High School for Girls) ordered that their hair be cut. Nits were, and even today remain, a contentious subject, and angry scenes took place outside the school. Mothers demonstrated and one woman, so it is said, poured a jug of syrup over Dr Rose's head. The Middle School pupils forgathered in the Gallowgate and staged a strike which lasted all afternoon. A crowd of Middle loons went down to Causewayend and banged on the windows, urging their comrades to show solidarity. Some of the younger Cassie-end boys came out in sympathy but the powers that be were not impressed by their industrial action and reprisals were duly exacted when they returned to school the following day.

Many older Cassie-enders speak of the sound quality of the education they received, and although there may have been poor living conditions at home, at school pupils enjoyed occasional red letter days with drawing and painting exhibitions in the upper hall, singing and dancing in the lower hall, trips to the fish market, the seaside, and the Art Gallery. The young Alberto Morocco, one of Scotland's most distinguished painters, attended Causewayend Primary, as it became after the First World War, before going on to Sunnybank Intermediate, and to Gray's School of Art, where he arrived as a fourteen-year-old! A favourite shop just beside the school was the famous Bendelow's bakery. Norah Morrison recalls that at breaktime Bendelow's sold pies to the pupils through a window which opened on to the playground. 'The girls' playground was nearest and the boys would give you a penny to buy them a pie. They'd usually give you a bit of the crust as well, in return.' This early takeaway also sold half pies for a halfpence.

During the last war Causewayend like many other Aberdeen schools, initially operated morning and afternoon 'shifts' and air raid drill was carried out. The worst moment came in April 1943, the day after the great raid which had created havoc in the area and wrecked Causewayend Church The school log reported that over 120 pupils were left homeless. Within a day or two, however, it recorded more cheerfully: 'the blitzed pupils are now returning to school'. There was also the local 'enemy' to be contended with when Sunnybank School was requisitioned by the army and its pupils deployed to Causewayend. Cassie-enders regarded Mounthooly as their stamping ground, taking the Gallowgate under their aegis as well. Sunnybankers, on the other hand, were a foreign tribe from the Spital. But a degree of segregation was practised, the Sunnybankers had a part of Causewayend School put at their disposal, and there is no record of any bloodshed. Joan Gray (Mrs MacMillan), remembers a favourite teacher, Miss Dorothy Allan from this time. 'Causewayend was her first school. She was young, a breath of fresh air. Because of the war, all the teachers we'd had up till then were elderly.'

Causewayend pupils 1945. Courtesy, Mrs Joan MacMillan.

The post war years brought new problems; one, short-lived and welcome was the arrival of the shelter-breakers who in 1946 caused a great deal of noise and dust, but all for a good cause. The school roll was now 'much diminished', down to 635 as result of slum clearance. At least there was now room for a nursery class.

The roll had nose-dived to 300, when Mrs Flora Youngson became the first woman head in 1970 to the chant of 'granny heidie, granny heidie,' from her charges. During her twelve years at Causewayend she is remembered as combining just the right blend of authority and couthiness. The basics were never neglected, no child left school, she recalls, without being able to read, write and count. But she also was determined to give her pupils as wide a cultural background as possible, involving the whole school in a series of projects on the sea and the city. At that time Shell's school for Dutch children was located at Causewayend and while each of the four classes had their own teacher, they joined the rest of the school for music, art, and in the playground. Mrs Youngson took the Dutch children for English lessons.

This was an eventful era. 'Education in the city was at an all time high. Money was reasonably plentiful and we had a liberally minded Town Council and a caring and interested administration,' wrote Flora Youngson in her memoir, *Dominie's Daughter*. 'Then, alas,' she continued, 'in 1974, came the twin evils of recession and regionalisation' when the new education authority was understandably determined to upgrade the former county schools, though at the expense of city schools. The resulting cutbacks meant the loss of the cookery and gardening classes that she had introduced for both boys and girls. Additionally there was a flow of 'endless paper edicts from Woodhill House'. One such required the immediate removal of any flammable material stored in boiler rooms. As the janitor, Jimmy Thompson, whose family boasted four generations of Cassie-enders, commented; 'Aye, and fit am Ah tae dee wi a my coal?'

Mrs Youngson was in post just in time to find herself nicely positioned between the proverbial rock and the hard place; the construction of the Mounthooly roundabout and the threat of closure. For seven years school life was disrupted by roadworks which involved the duelling of the A946, routed past the front of the school, as well as the creation of the roundabout itself. However, the building was as sound as a bell, and the thick walls deafened much of the noise. In the midst of this uproar came a happy occasion, the school's centenary and celebrations included a concert in which former pupil Anne Brand sang, and Alberto Morocco presented a picture. Thinking that it would be a good idea to mark the occasion by flying a flag, Flora Youngson ventured up the dusty, creaking tower stairs to find that the old flagpole had rotted away. She requisitioned a replacement from the education department, possibly one of the more unusual requests that came its way. And thanks largely to her efforts, the school was listed as a building of historic interest at this time.

In 1980 the threat of closure became a reality. Because of the falling roll and the education department's need to retrench, Causewayend was one of nine city primaries on the 'hit list'. Mrs Youngson then led a hard-fought

Pupils at Causewayend at the time of the centenary. The janitor, Mr James Thompson, is centre back.

campaign against closure, stressing that Causewayend was a happy, close-knit school, the focal point of the local community. Plans to transfer the children to Hanover Street School were condemned in view of the difficult cross-country journey across busy roads it would entail. And the telling point was made that if the school did close, it was inevitable that the buildings would be vandalised, an unacceptable fate for a listed building. Parents, pupils and staff wrote hundreds of letters appealing to MPs, councillors and the media. Petitions were got up and parents picketed the education department's headquarters at Woodhill House. It was a day of triumph mingled with relief when the Secretary of State overruled the decision to close. In the event, it was King Street School which amalgamated with Hanover Street, its buildings taken over by an expanding RGIT.

A staff reunion held in March 1976, to mark the school's centenary. Mrs Flora Youngson is seated, right foreground. Courtesy, Mrs F Youngson.

The school continues to play an important role in the area. Mr Alistair P Mackay, former Head of Lumsden Primary has been head since 1989 and the roll now stands at over 200, with twenty children attending morning and afternoon nursery classes. The stark, overcrowded classrooms of the past have been replaced by bright and cheerful rooms and there is a very supportive parents' group. A long-standing association with the kirk continues. The Reverend Laurie Gordon takes assembly once a fortnight while the children cross to John Knox's for services at Christmas and the end of the summer term. The Dutch children have gone now, and space at the school has been allocated to a Social Work section. And though the coming of the Fire Station to King's Crescent has been looked upon with trepidation by some residents, improvements to the school's playing fields with safer access and better changing facilities are built-in improvements that come with the new complex. Causewayend School looks forward to a brighter future.

Causewayend was originally set up to provide schooling for the incomers in the developing areas between Spring Garden and Hutcheon Street, while the Middle School, Causewayend's contemporary and near neighbour, was established to educate the ever-increasing juvenile population in the slums around Broad Street and the Gallowgate. Before its coming, the little schools in the area, several of which were set up by the Reverend Abercromby Gordon of Greyfriars, were having difficulty in coping. One was Greyfriars Kirk's own school, located for a time in Canal Road; others were the school of John Knox's Kirk, Mounthooly, whose own foundation was largely attributable to Gordon, and the Porthill School, larger than the others, and built by Gordon, one of the greatest philanthropists Aberdeen has known. It lay about half way along the Gallowgate, on the east side, opposite Soapy Ogston's. Not to be confused with Dr Reith's later Porthill Sunday School, it was run by trustees rather than the kirk. There was also Gerrard Street School of John Knox Free Kirk and the East Parish Church School in St Paul Street. Finally, in the 1860s, Father John Comper and the sisters of the Society of St Margaret had established a school in Ferguson's Court in the Gallowgate, just south of the Porthill

Ferguson's Court, Gallowgate leading to St Margaret's Church and School.
Courtesy, St Margaret's Convent.

110

School. Both church and school were initially based in a large room, but by the 1870s, a high, handsome new school for boys, girls and infants had appeared in the forecourt of the new St Margaret's Episcopal Church. St Margaret's, as an Episcopalian school, would remain for some considerable time outwith the Board's jurisdiction, but most of the others, Porthill, Greyfriars, Gerrard Street and the East Parish School, were taken over almost immediately, the latter becoming St Paul Street School. This would have come as a relief to the bodies, principally the kirk, responsible for their upkeep, but as they stood, church schools and endowed schools all over town represented something of a challenge to the School Board. In a progress report of 1907, the Board's clerk, the eminent Thomas Hector pulled no punches :

Classrooms were almost unknown. Single schoolrooms, in which four or five classes and as many teachers shouted each other down all day long were the rule. The cleanliness of desks, benches, floors, walls was at a low ebb; cloakrooms for the children's use was undreamed of, and a teacher's room or lavatory did not exist. Playground space was found, for the most part in the adjoining street, and the closets in which the children were expected to practice personal decency were, in nearly every case, indescribably filthy. In almost every case, schools had to be re-floored, re-desked and re-furnished.

In spite of these takeovers, improvements and enlargements, the Board deemed that a new public school was required for the densely populated area 'somewhere in the neighbourhood of the Upperkirkgate'. Reid's Court in the Gallowgate, near Littlejohn Street, was chosen as the site. David Reid, a cabinetmaker, once had his house there (his daughter Jean was the sister-in-law of the ironfounder William McKinnon), but house and court were duly demolished and the Middle School was opened on November 19, 1877. It was the Board's fourth school, and like Causewayend, the building project had been a costly one, the site alone costing £2,654 out of a total of £8,184. It followed the usual pattern of a public school, with infants, juniors and seniors, but the choice of name is curious. By no stretch of the imagination was it in the middle of town, as the Central High Grade School would be when it opened in 1905. It was in the east end, though perhaps, at a pinch, it lay roughly in the middle of the Board's other schools, Causewayend, Commerce Street and Ferryhill. Had it been given the usual territorial designation, it would have been Gallowgate School and in the early days it was sometimes written as Gallowgate (Middle). But the area contained some of Aberdeen's worst slums, and it may be that the Board wanted to start the school off with a clean slate, distancing it, mentally if not geographically from the slum context, hence the 'upmarket' name.

The structure of the original block was curious, with narrow wooden stairs, and numerous doors. Entrances and corridors were not considered essential, at least not for a year or two. Surrounded by Gallowgate closes and houses on the Littlejohn Street side, the Middle was all but hidden to the passer-by and from the start was dogged by the usual quart into a pint pot syndrome. Built to accommodate 700 scholars, 800 were on the role within the first year. At one point 240 pupils were being taught in the same room, just like the bad old days, though the cynical could argue that attendance was irregular enough to offer continuing respite from over-crowding. The first headmaster, Thomas Hynd, had been transferred with his staff from Greyfriars School, which had now been taken over by the Board and amalgamated. Hynd was something of a Moaning Minnie, and in the early logs he expresses despair of his charges. The newly enrolled were 'a straggling lot', while the juniors were 'not easy to manage'. Moreover he had to contend with gang warfare in the Gallowgate, report-ing in February 1878 that, 'a war spirit exhibits this week between various schools in the district. Vexing and provoking'. By 1883, the peripatetic Hynd and his team were off to break in a new school, King Street, where in the next decade, they would have had the joys of teaching the infant Harry Gordon whose family had moved to Urquhart Road.

The Middle was fortunate in its next head, James C Barnett, a pioneer of modern education. Contemporary photographs reveal Hynd as a bit of a bully boy, while Barnett with his neat grey beard and glasses looks scholarly and benign. French and Latin had been studied by the seniors from early days, but Barnett introduced science, including the study of electricity and magnetism, making some of the equipment himself. Cook-ery, needlework, dancing, singing drawing, shorthand, even elocution made their appearance on the curriculum and in 1911, a housewifery flat was created where generations of Middle girls, much to their enjoyment, could practice the skills of running a home and caring for a family. There was a phenomenon, too, the pupil James Mackenzie who was blind, yet did well in spite of his handicap, performing rather better on his typewriter than many of his sighted peers .

There were numerous improvements during the Barnett era; in 1901 came the first enlargement, making over 460 new places available, and a state of the art ventilation system, just like the one in the Palace Hotel, no less; halfpenny school meals were introduced around this time and in 1910, the Coats' of Paisley, the future Lord and Lady Glentanar, who were helping to fund the new John Knox's Church at Mounthooly, provided free schoolbags for all Middle scholars. A second, major programme of im-provements which began in 1907, entailed the removal of Union, Inglis' and

Ewen's Court in the Gallowgate, behind which the school sheltered. Indeed, the mighty 'Strathcona Hall' made its fleeting appearance on the vacant ground thus created, at the time of Aberdeen University's Quatercentenary celebrations. The familiar Gallowgate frontage was built at this time, inspired by the magnificent new Marischal College facade. Mr W Ogg Allan, architect and master of works to Aberdeen School Board was determined to create something worthy of the Middle's new neighbour that would be complementary yet restrained. If the Marischal frontage was over-the-top Gothic, the new Middle frontage was down-to-earth Gothic, plain, strong, with a sense of grace and that 'feeling of appropriateness' that Ogg Allan had striven for.

A spacious gym was added and 'a neat house' in the playground for the janitor', but the highlight of these extensions, the Board's great pioneering achievement, was the Middle Pond, as it was known in the early days. The Board had been accused of extravagance, and taken a great deal of 'stick'. Whoever heard of an east end school having a swimming pool? Board members stuck to their guns, however, and hailed its opening as 'a red letter

A view of the Middle School during demolition work at the Gallowgate. Note the original school buildings extreme left.

day in the history of Aberdeen School Board'. And so it was. The point was made that neighbouring schools, Causewayend, Porthill and St Paul Street would share in these new facilities, but pupils throughout the city were able to have lessons at the Middle Swimming Pool. Contrary to popular belief, the first instructor to be appointed in 1909 was Allan Brown, and not the immortal Mr Pirie who later taught generations of Aberdonians how to swim. I still recall a group of us making momentous journeys to the Middle after school on dreich Thursday afternoons when the lights of the town were just coming on. Neatly kitted out in nap coats and black velour hats, embellished with school badge and ribbon, we ran the gauntlet of the previous class, which consisted of rough boys who cried 'High School quines' after us. And there was Mr Pirie, red-faced and wiry, in shorts and sandals, his pole and whistle at the ready. In those days we had never seen an adult male so curiously attired. Yes, the Middle School provided one culture shock after another...but I am running too far ahead. The Middle had a good reputation in other sports too, with annual pupil-teacher competitions in cricket and football taking place annually as early as 1891. Basketball was played as well.

James Barnett retired in 1912, and was succeeded by William Thompson, in whose penultimate year, 1919, that the notorious hair-cutting episode already referred to took place. The extract from his log is worth quoting:

This has been a week of extreme difficulty. As a protest against the school medical officer cutting the hair of certain verminous children, an excited mob smashed with stones 500 panes of glass in the windows facing the north, The supposition was that Dr Rose was in the building at the time. The trouble came to a head by stone-throwing, fortunately after the children had been dismissed. The riotous conduct did not cease till after midnight on Monday.

Disruption, Thompson complained, continued through the week, 'mainly due to bands of pupils on sympathetic strike, and intermittent stone-throwing from lads of the hooligan type'.

In 1924, the Middle became an Intermediate School, and later a Junior Secondary, providing secondary education for twelve to fourteen-year-olds drawn from Causewayend, St Paul Street, Porthill and St Margaret's Episcopal. The school leaving age was raised to 15 in 1948 and the headmasters of those days kept a careful watch on bright children and late developers, encouraging them to continue their education at the Central Senior Secondary. If such a pupil was from a poor home, the 'heidie' ensured that grant aid would be available. One of the best and best-remembered headmasters of the modern era was Alfred Eddie, the school's

Pupils of room 13, 1948 - 49. Joan Gray is seated 2nd left, front row.
Courtesy, Mrs Joan MacMillan.

principal teacher of maths and science, and head from 1933 until his retirement in 1952. He did have a drawback, however. He was a dab hand with the tawse. The tale is told of the hapless pupil who came across from neighbouring St Paul Street School with a message and joined a queue outside the head's door with the aim of delivering it, unaware that his new companions were awaiting their scuds. The St Paul lad unfortunately got a totally undeserved belting. However, as I write, Mr Eddie's great-niece is preparing this book for publication, so I shall say no more about this notorious disciplinarian for the time being.

Another well-remembered head, and one of the last, was Alistair G Mackenzie. Clearances in the Gallowgate that had begun in the late nineteenth century continued well into the twentieth. The schools, like the churches, found their numbers diminishing. Porthill School, which back in 1878 had amalgamated with John Knox, Gerrard Street, closed in 1939, and St Margaret's Episcopal took over the building as an Infants' School. St Margaret's itself closed in 1959 and St Paul Street, in 1960. The Middle closed its doors in 1975, to the genuine regret of many of its former pupils who still look back with affection on their school days recalling the high standard of teaching. Former pupils still keep in contact and Joan Gray, who moved on to the Middle from Causewayend, has organised two highly successful reunions of the 'Class of 1946-49', in 1989 and again in 1994.

*Middle School friends
Margaret Imray and
Patsy Groat in 1948.*

*Together again, Patsy and Margaret left, with
Francis Reid and Isobel Bisset at the 1994 reunion.
Photographs, Courtesy, Mrs Joan MacMillan.*

Members of staff were recalled in a poem written to mark the latter occasion.

*We'd a fine team o' teachers - strict discipline the rule.
Baldie Eddie wis the 'Heidy', an naebody's fool...*

*Miss Berry taught Science; for English - Miss Blair.
Goofy Gordon, Miss Henfield, an' a good puckle mair...*

Nor was Mr Pirie and his Pool forgotten.

*Our school wis posh, wi a Pool - fit a dream!
It wis a mannie ca'd Peerie that learned us tae sweem.
We donned oor costumes, intae the water stepped doon
wi a rope 'neath oor oxters sae that we widna droon.*

116

The Middle building went on the market in 1981. There were several false starts when the site was sold for flats or office development, subject to planning permission, which for one reason or another was not forthcoming. For years the school remained a sad sight, its windows boarded up, surrounded by the wasteland created by the construction of the Bon Accord Centre. Eventually one offer was acceptable, and the school was demolished in the early 1990s. Prior to redevelopment, the city's keeper of archaeology, Judith Stones and her team, investigated. They discovered leather belt fragments, scraps from antler working, and a broken wooden paddle on the site. About fifty mediaeval boots and trimmings from shoemaking suggested that cobblers were working there by the early thirteenth century. A photographic record was made, and Miss Stones' slides reveal the skeleton of the 'pond' still dominating the foundations. More recent tokens of the school's existence seem to be in short supply. Barry Craigmile, technical director of W McKinnon & Co, remembers his art class painting a collage of West North Street and Mounthooly when the area was still a hive of industry; he has been unable to trace this vital historical record. Joan Gray too notes that the whereabouts of school's swimming trophies are presently unknown, disappointing, in view of the Middle's fame in this field.

A group of handsome flats has now arisen on the old site. Granite down-takings have been used to good effect and the gables of the new complex reflect, rather grandly, the silhouette of the old school.

Part Four

Life and Work

Pawnbroker's Sign, Porthill

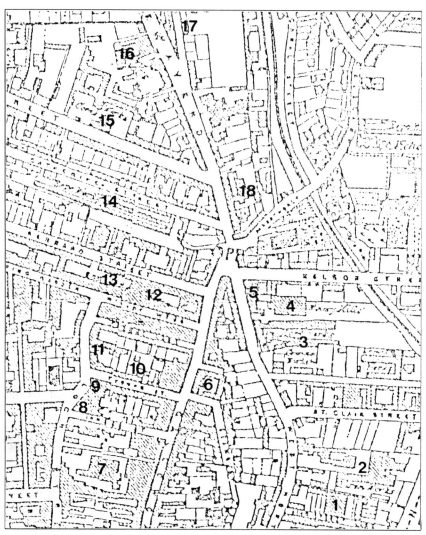

The Post Office Directory Map of 1880 has been used to plot the main industries around Mounthooly discussed in Chapters 9 and 10. There were also numerous granite yards.

1. John M Henderson. 2. Barry, Henry & Co. 3. Gray Watt's Ropeworks.
4. D Mackie's Wincey Mills. 5.Mulco. 6. The Porthill Factory. 7.'Soapy' Ogston's.
8. Aberdeen Dye Works. 9. Lochside Brewery. 10. Mulco, Barron & McAllan.
11. D Macandrew & Co. 12. W McKinnon. 13. Bell & Robertson.
14. Wm Routledge's Ropeworks. 15.Aberdeen Comb Works. 16. City Flour Mill
17. R G Garvie. 18. Munro's Transport.

Chapter 9

Industry: North Street to Loch Street

Anyone who has tried to find out about Aberdeen's traditional industries will have faced difficulties. Facts are scattered and photographs almost as rare as hens' teeth.
Mechanical Aberdeen, John S Reid, 1990

Industry had been attracted to the area around the Gallowgate-head long before the coming of the turnpike. Here, on the edge of town there was space to expand, yet it was within easy walking distance of the city centre - Broad Street and the Castlegate. As the nineteenth century progressed, the Gallowgate-head, or Mounthooly as it was sometimes now called, became increasingly industrialised, though it retained a flavour of the country for many years.

Nowhere was this more evident than in West North Street, that 'B road' on Gordon's Plan of 1661. The Back Causeway, as it used to be known, ran behind the gallows and the Porthill windmill, passing the Back Butts on the east and the Marischal College garden on the west before reaching the north side of the Castlegate. By the eighteenth century, the Back Causeway had become North Street, an important link between the Gallowgate-head and points north, and the Quay.

It was a busy street, a place of inns and stables, smithies and forges. The meal and poultry markets were situated almost opposite the College garden, 'both being laid out on excellent plans' as William Kennedy reports in his *Annals of Aberdeen* (1818). Butter and cheese were sold there, 'brought to the town from almost every part of this extensive county'. Kennedy

121

noted 'a daily supply of vegetables of all kinds' and a 'great abundance' of potatoes. During the season, 'immense quantities of strawberries, gooseberries, and other small fruit are brought to the market almost daily' a fair proportion, one would guess, coming from nurseries no great distance away, around Mounthooly. A gardener could make £1000 annually from his strawberries and gooseberries, a very reasonable return for his labours in those days. Mealmarket Lane, later widened and promoted to Street grew up on this site, linking North Street and King Street, while the meal and poultry markets became redundant with the opening of Archibald Simpson's spectacular New Market in 1842.

Mealmarket Street, from an old painting.

By the late eighteenth century, North Street was also developing as an 'industrial complex'. Joseph Rowell Snr was established there, his surname indicating that he could have come from as far afield as Devon to ply his craft. He was a blacksmith to trade though Aberdeen's first post office directory of 1824-25 lists him as a chainmaker. The building of sailing ships was approaching its zenith, so it seems that he had discovered a profitable specialism. He lived virtually over the shop, in Littlejohn's Street (after a local property owner, William Littlejohn), then later round in Longacre, whose site these many years has lain under the south side of Marischal College. In Rowell's day, Longacre was not the slum that it was at the time of its demise, and at one time he may have had the distinguished architect, John Smith, as a neighbour.

The post office directory of 1828 shows another Joseph Rowell, prob-

122

ably his son, working as a chainmaker on his own account. He has not strayed far from the family home, only the length of Mealmarket Lane. By 1832 - if not earlier for the post office directory was inevitably in arrears - other members of the Rowell family were also making their way as chainmakers, but the younger Joseph has branched out and turned his Mealmarket Lane premises into a comb factory. He even has a partner outwith the family circle, John Stewart, another Longacre resident. Stewart & Rowell, combmakers, were in business.

Until this time, combs were made on a 'one off' basis by itinerant artisans. In 1825, however, the forward-looking Stewart had started up a combworks in Edinburgh though it seems not to have flourished. Three years later the mass production of combs became more feasible when a twinning machine, which simultaneously cut two combs out of one plate of horn, was invented by a Mr Lynn. Stewart decided to try his luck in Aberdeen and found in Joseph Rowell a man with technical expertise, suitable premises and an entrepreneurial outlook. At Mealmarket Lane, Stewart and Rowell prospered. They were able to employ a workforce of around forty and to install a steam engine, a source of power that was still a novelty.

Nearby, at the King Street end of North Street, was the yard of the Perthshire-born mason Alexander Macdonald, then in his late twenties. Here he wrought mantelpieces, headstones and paving stones in marble and freestone. On learning that the British Museum was displaying newly acquired specimens of ancient Egyptian polished granite, Macdonald made the historic decision to travel to London to see them. It is said that Aberdeen's great trade in polished granite dates from the moment that young Alexander gazed enraptured at the masterpieces of the Pharaohs. Be that as it may, on his return to North Street he succeeded in reviving the ancient skill of polishing granite. It had to be done by hand, however, and although the results were excellent, the process was slow and impracticable.

Macdonald persevered. He asked for, or was invited to have a 'shot' of the combworks' steam engine. It would have been of the stationary variety, and whether it was able to provide power directly from the combworks to the granite yard by belts and pulleys, whether it was conveyed to Macdonald's yard and bolted down again, or whether he carted round samples of granite, it is impossi-

Alexander Macdonald.

123

ble to tell. It would have depended on how close the two premises were. Whatever the *minutiae* of the story, Macdonald's first attempt to polish granite by machinery was successfully achieved with the assistance of the combworks' steam engine. He now invented his own dressing and polishing machinery and by 1832, a tombstone of beautifully polished Aberdeenshire granite from the North Street yard was creating much interest in Kensal Green Cemetery, London, the first such memorial to be found in an English cemetery. The trade in monumental masonry now took off. Machinery became more sophisticated and in the early years of the twentieth century when the industry was at its peak, as many as ninety Aberdeen yards were employing a workforce of around 2000. Back in the mid-1830s, Alexander Macdonald, enjoying the first fruits of success, had left North Street and opened a bigger yard at Constitution Street. While his products commemorated the dead, those of his neighbours, John Stewart and Joseph Rowell continued to titivate the living. Soon they would too would be on their travels.

Heading now along North Street, the ironworks of David Carter, machine-maker, boilermaker and general blacksmith were to be found some distance north of the junction with Mealmarket Lane. A pioneer of engineering and iron founding in the north of Scotland, Carter had established his business in 1794, soon after the discovery of new deposits of iron ore gave an impetus to the skill. Until that time, the Carron Ironworks, set up in 1759, had cornered all available supplies.

Time passed, and by the 1850s, Carter's site was acquired for rather different purposes by Dickson, Hogarth & Co, preserved provision merchants. Their principal factory was in College Street and the West North Street site - the 'West' was now in use - was used as a boilyard, doubtless to the chagrin of neighbours. Several members of the Hogarth family were in this business, and one of them, William, 'provision curer and merchant', had set up a whaling concern, the Aberdeen Arctic Company in 1854, which enjoyed moderate success. No doubt additional capacity was required for processing whale and seal meat.

In just over a decade, the whaling company was wound up and the site was eventually taken over by the Aberdeen Foundry of Barry, Henry & Co. They flitted from their Loch Street fastness where they had, for many years, combined ironfounding with the manufacture of manure from bones. The latter line was not pursued in West North Street, thus sparing residents a fresh round of smells. Of the principals, Barry is an enigma, but George Henry was a kenspeckle figure. A bachelor, he was provost from 1850-52, and Henry Street was named in his honour. Lachlan Mackinnon has provided a memorable pen portrait in his *Recollections of an Old Lawyer*:

He was the last in Aberdeen to use hair powder. We could see the powder as we looked down (from the church gallery) on his venerable pate. He was a good-looking, stately old man who made a fine figure among the elders ...His neck was surrounded by such a wealth of white linen that he was known familiarly as 'The British Linen Company'.

'The British Linen Company' alias Provost Henry of Barry, Henry & Co.

Such affectations are not normally associated with the 'hands on' ironfounder. His attendance at Napoleon III's Great Exhibition prompted David Finlay, overseer to Lord James Hay of Seaton, to write to his employer, at that time domiciled in Paris: 'Have you happened to meet our Lord Provost Henry at the Paris Festivities? I think his appearance with his powdered head may attract some notice'.

From the 1830s, however, it had been William Henderson, who lived in Loch Street, virtually over the shop, who was involved in the management of Barry, Henry. The ownership, at the time of Provost Henry's death in 1867, was vested in Miss Barry and Mrs Trail, possibly Barry's daughters, but William Henderson eventually became sole partner. By the time the business moved to West North Street, he had quitted his house in Loch Street for Ardeir, Mannofield, which is remembered as the home, rather later, of the comedian, Harry Gordon.

In 1889, Mr Charles Cook and his son, Robert bought the firm from William Henderson and took over as chairman and managing director respectively. Charles Cook, born in Frederick Street where his family had been in the stagecoach business, was not an engineer to trade - though two of his sons were - but a hotelier, a farmer and an Aberdeen county councillor. Charles and Robert Cook revitalised the works, building an engineering shop, four-storeys high, said to be one of the finest in Scotland.

In December 1890, the *Aberdeen Journal*, in describing the premises, revealed how a well-stocked foundry of the time should be fitted out. The engine shop, 250 feet by 80 feet and supported by massive cast iron pillars had been designed by the foreman of the works, Mr Alexander Guild. It contained numerous machines of the most modern American make, including a wheel cutting machine, the largest of its kind, turning out 200 to 300 feet of shafting a day, as well as belt and rope pulleys, gearing and shaft-

The engine shop at Barry, Henry & Cook.

bearings, products for which the firm became well known. At one end of this shop, 'a large staff of blacksmiths' were busy manufacturing pitch chains, destined for Kensal Green, though the gasworks rather than the cemetery. Beyond the engineering shop was the foundry yard, with great stores of moulding boxes, pig-iron and coke. Nearby three cupolas were in operation for melting iron, 'one for chilled castings, another for medium castings, the third for heavy work'. A railway connected the foundry to the engine room. Powerful overhead travelling cranes were everywhere. The millwright department was located on the second floor where water wheels and threshing mills were made, while 'all sorts of patterns' were stored in the two floors above. There was even a department with 'an immense stock of wrought iron pulleys, bolts, steel keys, beltings and fixing.' Truly, a Victorian iron founder's delight. The workforce was around 200.

The Cook name was not added to Barry, Henry until 1920, some two years after Charles Cook's death. His son, Robert briefly survived him but by the mid-1920s it was the third generation in the person of the young R C V Cook, who took over as managing director. It is said that during those difficult years, his widowed mother, Mrs Robert S Cook, was much involved in the running of the firm, and with obvious success, for in the 1930s, mother and son left their home in King's Gate for the palatial Countesswells House where Victor Cook remained for the rest of his long life. Many tales could be told of this altruistic industrialist. Senior members of the workforce, for example, were given assistance to buy their own houses, the loans repayable at very low rates of interest.

The firm continued to expand, making castings for bridges, building

The iron foundry, later to be occupied by Barry, Henry & Co, sits in open fields between King Street and West North Street. From the George Washington Wilson Bird's Eye View of 1850.

structures and municipal works, as well as small steam engines and much else. In more recent times, plant was manufactured and exported to Europe and beyond, while the foundry specialised in the supply of alloy and high duty irons.

By 1880, Barry, Henry had a new neighbour, immediately to the south, the King's Works of John M Henderson & Co Ltd. The two engineering firms lay somewhat incestuously side by side, both in L-shaped buildings. Henderson's front office, as the name implies, was in King Street but the works went through to West North Street. The foundry was beside the old North Lodge, now Victoria House. The Hendersons were a rather more ill-fated family than the Cooks. John Henderson, father of the founder and a

127

noted lithographer, was killed when he fell down a lift shaft in the Union Buildings where he had his business. At that time, his son, John M Henderson, born in 1843, was but a babe-in-arms. Later the young Henderson served his apprenticeship at James Abernethy's Ferryhill Iron Foundry, and after gaining further experience, set up on his own in a small way in Jopp's Lane near Spring Garden.

Henderson, according to his obituarist, was, 'an excellent type of the shrewd, enterprising, successful Aberdonian'. A prominent member of the Hammermen Incorporation, he kept an ear close to the ground, made it his business to know how various local industries were developing, and was always ready to supply their needs. Hence the blondin. This aerial suspension cableway was invented by the Kemnay quarry owner, John Fyfe, in 1872. The name had been inspired by Charles Blondin, whose memorable crossing of Golden Square by tightrope during his visit to Aberdeen in 1861 was still recalled. The blondin's capacity to lift stone from any part of the quarry made it a versatile rival to the old steam derrick. Within a few years John M Henderson was designing and manufacturing numerous aerial cableways to meet the demand from local quarriers, and the need for more space prompted the move to King Street. Moreover, blondins could be applied to a multiplicity of industrial uses, and one of Henderson's first tasks in the new premises was the manufacture of a cableway required for the erection of Kew Bridge over the Thames.

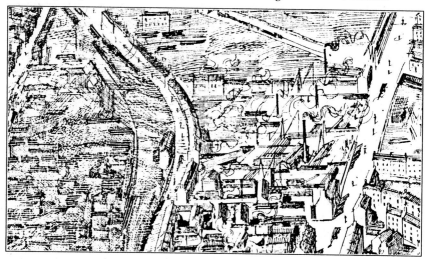

A hive of industry between West North Street to the left and King Street to the right. The white gable-end in King Street marks the junction with Mealmarket Street. Just beyond are the engineering works of John M Henderson, with those of Barry, Henry & Co behind them. From the lithograph of 1889 by Andrew Gibb & Co.

128

At a later date, Henderson cableways were used in the construction of hydro-electric dams and reservoirs all over the world. The firm specialised in all manner of mechanical handling equipment, cranes, conveyors, suspension bridges, heists, slipways, haulage plants, electric furnaces. Between the wars, they constructed five great aerial cableways to transport materials used in the construction of the Nag Hammadi Barrage over the Nile; they carried out canal and dock construction in Holland; they built a complete coaling, storage, and reclaiming plant at Port Royal, Jamaica, dock works in Turkey, cranes for the shipbuilders, Harland & Wolff, coke oven machinery for Australia. In 1955 they designed and manufactured ten electrically operated passenger lifts for new piers at Hong Kong and Kowloon. The world was their oyster and in Aberdeen, the massive fitting-up and assembly shops stretching between King Street and West North Street were a sight to see.

The Hendersons themselves had not lived to enjoy such great success. John M Henderson, 'the most genial of men' had died suddenly in 1900 at the age of 57. He was succeeded by his son, John M Henderson Jnr whom he had assumed as partner only two years earlier. On the sudden death of the younger John M Henderson and his wife in 1924, a brother-in-law, Edwin Taggart, son of Lord Provost Sir James Taggart took over the management of the firm.

Three years earlier, in 1921, Richard E Spain, who would become one of the firm's 'greats', had joined Henderson's as office boy. By 1945 he would be managing director, renowned for his world-wide travels to secure orders for the firm. This he carried out with conspicuous success, even behind the Iron Curtain during the time of the Cold War. Richard Spain was following an essential tradition of the firm. As early as 1900, one of John M Henderson Snr's sons was in Tasmania on company business at the time of his father's death, indicating awareness, even at that time, that Henderson's skills as engineers had to be complemented by the ability to sell their products in the burgeoning markets of the world.

The third engineering firm in West North Street, Mulco Products, started up at the Nelson Street end, backing on to the 'Globie', and was quite different in its origins from the others. Adolf Muller, born in Breslau, Germany in 1876, served an apprenticeship as a botanical gardener in Berlin, came to Britain, where he worked first at Kew Gardens, then in Aberdeen with William Smith & Son at their Burnside nurseries. Young Muller explored the North East and spotted a gap in the market for the supply of agricultural machinery, a product he was well placed to import since his father-in-law owned an agricultural machine factory in Breslau. In 1905 he set up at No 184 West North Street as A Muller & Co, (soon

Mulco's imported washing machines, left, and butter churns, right, on display .
Courtesy, Ernest Muller.

abbreviated to Mulco), seed merchants and importers of agricultural implements - grain lifters, tattie diggers, muck spreaders, and much else. In addition the firm manufactured a patented item, the Muller Pole Point and Carrier at West North Street, a 'best-seller' which provided easier draft and steering for horse drawn agricultural machinery. Adolf Muller was an 'over the shop' man with a vengeance. The family at that time lived next door to the 'Globie', and Ernest Muller, the firm's present managing director, remembers his father knocking a door through on the landing of their home to give direct access to his office.

Mulco widened its field of operations to include the importation of milk cans, butter churns, washing machines and operated an agency for Adler motor cars and motor cycles. Adolf Muller had became a naturalised British subject in 1913, and during the First World War, the firm, the first sheet metal working establishment in the North East, manufactured watertight hatches for the Admiralty and mudguards for the Army. Always adaptable and innovative, apt at finding gaps in the market, Mulco later increased its range, developing bakery equipment, including a flour sifter, which led to the wider field of powder sifting and the manufacture of powder handling equipment.

Over the years the firm occupied a number of premises around Mounthooly, in Spring Garden, Young Street and Willowdale Place off West North Street where Ernie Muller remembers they had a sawmill as a neighbour. In 1954, however, Mulco, moved to St Machar Road where all

Adolf Muller with one of the Adler motors. Courtesy Ernest Muller.

operations were subsequently gathered under one roof. Adolf Muller himself had died in 1953 and was succeeded as head of the firm by Ernest, an engineering graduate of Aberdeen University who saw service with the RAF during the war. The third generation of Mullers, Ernest's son Michael, joined the firm as an engineering apprentice in 1960 and became a partner in 1965.

Over the years, numerous industries were to be found in West North Street including a brewery, and John Harper's Ironworks, which later moved to Craiginches. Near the Mounthooly end, the ropeworks of Gray, Watt & Co, were set up in 1780, and remained there for a century and a half. The ropewalk is shown on Wood's Map on page 14, above James Roy's nursery, with a lane alongside, giving access to the Aberdeenshire Canal. In the early nineteenth century Gray, Watt were involved in the dressed hemp and flax trade, and later specialised in manufacturing all kinds of ropes, twines, fishing lines and nets. 'The line trade was greatly developed about 1835 by Mr John Duncan, the grandfather of the present proprietor who many times went to Russia and selected the raw material on the spot', *Aberdeen Today* reported in 1907. In 1884 the firm had redeveloped on the same site, building a sizeable warehouse and extending the ropewalk to meet the railway below the Nelson Street bridge.

If Gray, Watt had eroded a part of Roy's Nursery, its neighbour immediately to the north swallowed up the rest. This was the West North Street Factory, the wincey and linen factory of David Mackie & Co, established in 1860s, later and more genteelly, the Nelson Mills, a neighbour of Mulco's. The firm originally had a retail outlet in St Nicholas Street, but the factory continued long after the shop changed hands. Indeed it remained on the same site, behind the 'Globie' until the 1950s.

Moving round Mounthooly in a clockwise direction, we cross now to the Porthill Factory at 'Seamount, Gallowgate-head'. It was built in 1752 for the Porthill Company whose venture soon failed, and in 1763, Milne, Cruden & Co, linen manufacturers, took over the premises. Milne, Cruden who already owned a spinning mill and bleachfield at Gordon's Mills, in common with other Woodside mill owners, were landed gentlemen, often related through marriage and sometimes dabbling in politics. Of the named principals, the Milnes were lairds of the Buchan estate of Crimonmogate, while Provost William Cruden's main claim to fame was largely vicarious. A relative, Alexander, had compiled 'Cruden's Concordance' to the Bible, famous in his day and long after.

A few years after taking over the Porthill Factory, Milne Cruden built a new mill across on the Spring Gardens-Lochside corner where advantage could be taken of two sides of the lade which turned there to flow south towards the Loch-Eye. Milne's Plan of 1789 below, shows the Porthill Factory, marked 'Messrs Milne, Cruden & Co, Factory', while the nearby Spring Garden Works are marked '10'. The neighbouring factory, marked '11', was owned by a Mr Jessamine.

Although the Spring Garden Works were custom-built, conditions were among the worst of the town's factories, particularly for those young

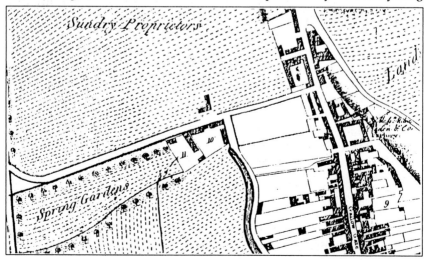

A detail from Milne's Plan of 1789.

132

The Spring Garden Works of Milne, Cruden & Co in Loch Street, photographed in the 1980s, prior to demolition. The gable end, right, turns into Spring Garden.

girls and women involved in wet spinning. Their frocks or coarse linen aprons would be soaked by spray from the spindles; water on the stone floors gave them the option of standing in soaking shoes or going barefoot in the wet and the dirt. In the hot, wet spinning department, conditions were even more desperate, with the dangers of constant steam, and temperatures of over 100°F to be endured. Long hours were worked, and though plagued by coughs, sore throats and rheumatics, the women were fined if absent through illness. Fortunately conditions improved following the passing of the 1833 Factory Act, particularly with regard to child labour. By the 1840s, however, the textile industry was in a depression and on April 17 1849, there was put on the market to be sold or let:

> The Extensive Square of Stone Buildings known as the Porthill Factory situated near Gallowgate-head, and for many years past occupied as a Flax Manufactory by Messrs Milne Cruden & Company. The Premises might be used as a Manufactory as formerly, or as Warehouses, for which they are well adapted. A Purchaser might find it in his interests to erect a range of Dwelling houses and shops, with fronts to the Gallowgate and Porthill, and looking on one side towards the sea.

This *Aberdeen Journal* advertisement rounds off in true estate agent style: 'The situation is elevated and airy, and the neighbourhood recently improved'.

It was Samuel Willans, stoneware manufacturer, already in residence as a tenant, who took over the Porthill Factory. His home and business had earlier been in West North Street, and he must have looked up at the towering pile every day. He seems to have done well, for he was able to move to the house of Friendly Bank, Mounthooly, where he continued to live after his retirement. As for Milne, Cruden & Co, they were out of business altogether by 1854. The Spring Garden Works were closed and the premises spent the rest of their days as a store.

Three little streets just south of Spring Garden dipped down to link the Gallowgate and Loch Street. Young Street, the middle of the three, was laid out on ground owned by Milne, Cruden & Co. In 1806, the Police Commissioners, then responsible for roads and paving, were pleased to agree to a suggestion by the company that a short street be opened opposite the Porthill Factory, linking, the Gallowgate and the Lochside and creating a useful access to nearby John Street, the most important of the new Lochlands streets, bar George Street. It was probably named after Alexander Young of Cornhill, Milne, Cruden's managing partner and the 'Mr Fixit' who had initially acquired the Porthill Factory on behalf of his colleagues.

Young Street, small though it was, had its own industries. Milne's Preserved Provision Works started up its first jam factory there; the Bon-

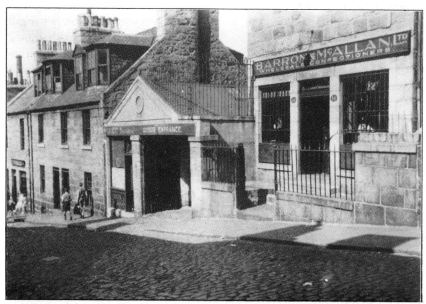

Mulco's premises in Young Street, centre, in the 1930s, with Barron & McAllan, wholesale confectioners, right. Courtesy, Ernest Muller.

134

Accord Bacon and Ham Factory was making its presence felt by the end of the nineteenth century, followed by Barron & McAllan, wholesale confectioners. From the 1930s, Mulco Ltd, manufactured bakery equipment there, next door to Barron & McAllan.

In 1850 Daniel Macandrew established his Steam Joinery and Building Works at the junction of Young Street and Loch Street, a corner which originally would have been on the Lochside. This firm is best remembered for its carpentry, but often acting as builders and principal contractors had many strings to its bow. It carried out pioneering work in concrete on the Jute Street-King's Crescent corner in 1875, building a group of interesting houses which are now Category-B listed. A few years later, however, death, disaster, fire, even flood for all we know - the Loch has a habit of returning - overtook the firm. To the rescue came a former apprentice J A Smith, who had gained much useful experience in London. He rebuilt the premises in granite, three storeys high, and acquired extra ground all around. Sole contractors for 'H M Convict Prison, Peterhead', D Macandrew & Co, appropriately enough, now went on to build Craiginches Prison. But the firm's talents were by no means confined to the demands of penal servitude. A number of interestingly varied contracts were completed, including the building of the Palm House in the Duthie Park or the 'Hot House' as it was called in my young day. It was bulldozed in 1969 to make way for the present Winter Gardens.

The legendary, if fleeting, 'Strathcona Hall' was one of the firm's most celebrated structures. In the course of a week in September 1906, Aberdeen University marked its quatercentery, the principal event being the inaugu-

Strathcona Hall

ration by King Edward V11 of the magnificent Marischal College extensions. Macandrew & Co, working to designs by the architect A Marshall Mackenzie, had, in six weeks, constructed and furnished a vast hall stretching from Marischal College north along vacant ground in the Gallowgate, cleared to make way for extensions to the Middle School. According to the quartercentenary programme it appears to have been used twice, once for a reception for around 5000 guests, once for a banquet for 2500 dignitaries. It was then dismantled and the site cleared in ten days. Lord Strathcona, Chancellor of Aberdeen University, footed the bill, £3,400, a sizeable sum at that time. Given the slum conditions which prevailed in the Gallowgate, the money might have been better spent, and the new Mitchell Hall used for the functions instead. But possibly it was not large enough. On a smaller scale, the firm produced several ranges of school desks, whose wrought iron work ornamented by the letter M, an early example of the advertising logo, would have been supplied by one of the neighbourhood foundries. Macandrew's craftsmen were also responsible for the superb wooden panelling in the University Court Room in Marischal College, and for the Austrian wainscot in the 'public office' of the then magnificent new Scots baronial post office building Crown Street. They also built some fine church organ cases.

A Macandrew desk. Note the 'M'.

South of Young Street was Innes Street, laid out in 1813. My candidate for the eponymous Mr Innes was the founder, circa 1800, of the Aberdeen Dye Works which, like Macandrew's, stood at the Loch Street end, well-positioned to take advantage of the Lochside lade, as was its more extensive northerly neighbour, the Lochside Brewery. That at least would have been the case in the early days. The water of the lade was suspect at the best of times, and the dye works' situation downstream of the brewery meant that the quality of the water available would not be of the most choice. By 1889, however, a report on the company in *Scotland of Today* was stressing its use of water from the River Dee 'which cannot be surpassed for cleaning and dyeing purposes'. As the nineteenth century progressed, the lade became redundant, thanks to vast improvements in the water supply and the availability of steam power.

The Aberdeen Dye Works, which by 1889 had agencies throughout Scotland and 'in all parts of London', had moved with the times and boasted 'a splendidly appointed receiving-room' and a spacious dye-house with six enormous vats, while the drying department on the second floor was a power house buzzing with the noise of hydraulic presses, metal-cased steam drums, rapid running mangles and glazing machinery. Given current embargoes on suitability of various materials for dyeing, the range of garments tackled by Aberdeen Dye Works was most impressive. As well as run-of-the-mill skirts, jackets, trousers, coats and dresses they would dye:

fur jackets, tweed waterproofs, quilten satin petticoats, woollen dressing gowns, shawls, shawlettes, veils, plaids, scarves, muffs, cuffs and collarettes, kid gloves, worsted stockings, ribbons, sofa blankets, linen floorcloths, silk, damasks, chintz, carpets, velvet, velveteen, muslin, leno (fine muslin), wincey and feathers which were cleaned and curled as well.

South of Innes Street, the Candle and Soap Works of Alex Ogston & Sons, later Ogston & Tennant, bestrode a sizeable area between Loch Street and the Gallowgate. After the Second World War, the firm was taken over by Unilver, a famous name but one which did not have quite the same homely ring about it as 'Soapy' Ogston's.

Turning back now, *en route* to Spring Garden and Windy Wynd, one would have passed Berry Lane, promoted to Street in the late nineteenth century, the oldest and most northerly of the three little thoroughfares. (A new street, part of the Bon-Accord Centre infrastructure, was named Berry Street in the early 1990s. It lies at the south end of the Gallowgate and was not the site of the original Berry Lane/Street). Unlike it neighbours, old Berry Street was not a hot bed of industry, but it could be a dangerous place in its day. Muggings are nothing new. On December 2, 1812, the *Aberdeen Journal* reported that:

About 9 o'clock at night a servant maid in coming up Berry Lane was, near the top of it, surrounded by three fellows who came from the Gallowgate. Two of them, after striking her in the most unmanly manner, robbed her forcibly of a bundle containing some wearing apparel, her Bible, and over £4 sterling, the amount of wages she had just received ...Two men came to her assistance and joined in pursuit of the villains who effected their escape across the Canal into a stockyard.

Our journey now moves north to look at the industries of Windy Wynd, Spring Garden and beyond.

Windy Wind and the Spring Garden Iron Works of William McKinnon & Co Ltd. towards the end of the nineteenth century, from the north end of Loch Street. It was here that the lade turned to flow south. The start of Spring Garden is shown left. Granite from the gables and the arch stones of the windows have been used for the student accommodation now occupying this site. Courtesy, William McKinnon & Co Ltd.

Chapter 10

Industry: Windy Wynd to Mounthooly

There is a crying need for thorough studies of Aberdeen's industry, which has enjoyed half-a-dozen romances.

A Thousand Years of Aberdeen, Alexander Keith, 1972

Like North Street, Windy Wynd and the Spring Gardens, near the town yet offering room for development, was a good place for industry to take root and flourish. There was the additional advantage of the lade, which had attracted the linen manufacturers, Milne, Cruden & Co, and others to the area. The lade was one of Aberdeen's earliest industrial aids, running north-east across town from the Gilcomston Dam to the Broadford Dam, providing power for a number of primitive mills on the way. In the Broadford Dam its waters mingled with those of the West Burn, and thus reinforced, but kept in about by bulwarks and saughs, the lade made it way along the Spring Gardens, turning at the junction with Windy Wynd to flow south along the Lochside, where other industries availed themselves of its services, and so to the Loch-Eye.

Across the road from Milne, Cruden's Spring Garden Works, near the Windy Wynd-Gallowgate corner was Watson's Foundry. Possibly the first in Aberdeen, it had been built around 1760 on croft land feued from King's College, and is clearly shown on Taylor's Plan of 1773. Watson's output must have been inhibited by the limited availability of iron ore, and he probably did little more than casual work for neighbouring mills and manufactories.

William McKinnon, founder of the firm aged 93. Courtesy, William McKinnon & Co Ltd.

By the early 1790s the discovery of new deposits of ore gave impetus to the industry, and in 1798, William McKinnon, the twenty-one-year-old son of a Greenock shipwright, set up a foundry next door to Watson's and presently took that firm over. McKinnon called his foundry the Spring Garden Iron Works, which had more of a ring about it than the topographically correct 'Windy Wynd Iron Works'. The firm prospered and expanded along the Spring Gardens, buying up the land between the Gallowgate and George Street in 50 feet strips.

William's eldest son, Lachlan McKinnon Snr, born 1811, served his legal apprenticeship and became an advocate in Aberdeen. He later gave up the law and took over the running of the foundry as managing partner. He was also a director of the Aberdeen Copper Company, (as was Provost Henry of Barry, Henry & Co), and that accounted for his nickname, 'Pots'. He was 'a Bohemian for his time, fond of books and music', and like Provost Henry, had an unconventional taste in attire, though unlike the Provost, he affected the style of Sherlock Holmes, wearing 'an Inverness cape and a soft hat at a time when to do so in Union Street was unusual'. The Mac/ McKinnons were a talented family. William, the ironfounder, was the younger brother of the shipmaster Lachlan Mackinnon (they used different spellings of the surname), who was the father of Lachlan Mackinnon Jnr, founder of the well known Aberdeen legal dynasty. That use of 'Junior' distinguished him from his non-practising cousin, 'Pots', who was eight years older. Lachlan Mackinnon, author of *Recollections of an Old Lawyer*, (to whom we are indebted for the description of Lachlan McKinnon Snr quoted above), was the son of Lachlan Mackinnon Jnr. William McKinnon died in 1873 at the age of ninety-five, the oldest man in Aberdeen, so it was said. 'Pots' had predeceased his father, and the firm was run by another son, John, along with the munificent Councillor John Gray and William Henderson, but not the William Henderson who ran Barry, Henry & Co.

The era from the 1790s, until the first half of the nineteenth century was one of great industrial activity in Aberdeen and McKinnon's supplied castings for factories and for agricultural

John Gray, ironfounder and donor of Gray's School of Art to the city

needs. However a change of direction came gradually, starting in 1857 when an Aberdonian, David Graeme Robertson, a contact of the McKinnon's, started up an engineering company in Kuala Lumpur. It was through him that the firm began to make and export coffee plantation machinery to Malaysia, as they do to this day. Four generations of Robertsons, three of them called David Graeme (just when we had got the Lachlan McKinnons and William Hendersons sorted out) would now be involved in running the firm. A former McKinnon apprentice, John Gordon, who was London-based by the 1860s, also appears on the scene, He too had contacts with the plantations - cocoa, sugar and rice as well as coffee - and as a result, McKinnons began to manufacture a range of plantation machinery for customers on a world-wide basis. By the early twentieth century, as an article on McKinnon's in the *Aberdeen Chamber of Commerce Journal* recalled: 'the concentration of Scotsmen, and particularly Aberdonians, in the plantations of Malaya, Indonesia, and the French preserves of Indo-China like Annam and Tonking, was remarkably thick and the field (for McKinnon's) to reap was ready at hand.'

After John McKinnon's death in 1885, John Gray, who two years earlier had gifted Gray's School of Art to the city, was joined on the board by John McKinnon's sons Chalmers and Frederick, and they, the grandsons of the founder, were at the helm when the firm reached its centenary in 1898. Not for much longer, however. By 1890, members of the Robertson family, one of whom had married a McKinnon, were on the board and in 1906 the firm became a private limited company in which the Robertsons were majority shareholders. They marked the beginning of their reign with a major reorganisation and revamp, which continued over some ten years. By 1907

The blacksmiths' shop at McKinnons early in the twentieth century. Courtesy, William McKinnon & Co Ltd.

the frontage had been extended from 740 feet to 1100 feet, along the Spring Garden, Gallowgate and Gerrard Street sides, and *Aberdeen Today* provided an enthusiastic 'write-up':

> The foundry, which is replete with all the latest appliances is capable of turning out 3000 tons of casting annually ...Messrs McKinnon & Co have a worldwide connection in the making of every description of steam engines and boilers, millwright work, sugar machinery, bone-crushing machinery, mining machinery and all apparatus for meat preserving.

The finishing touches to the Spring Garden Works were applied in 1916, when the architect George Coutts was instructed to rebuild the main office block in French Renaissance style. This explains why a section vaguely reminiscent of the Place des Vosges in Paris and surmounted by a wrought iron crown, used to sit a trifle uneasily amidst the no-nonsense vernacular of the Spring Garden frontage. Fine attention to detail was also provided at this time, with interesting art nouveau embellishment. An addition, not foreseen a few years earlier, came on the instruction of the Ministry of Munitions in 1917. During the First World War, McKinnons, like other local engineering firms, was heavily involved in warwork. So

The wrought iron crown. Courtesy, City of Aberdeen - Planning Division.

many shells were manufactured at Spring Garden that it was necessary to extend the shell bond room.

For its first hundred years and more, the work of the firm was wide-ranging, from, for example, the Fochabers Bridge in 1862, to supplying of water pipes for washing ore during the tin-mining boom in 1910. More space was required for pipe storage, hence the leasing of ground in Canal Road. During the twentieth century, however, McKinnon's increasingly specialised in the manufacture of equipment to process sugar, rice and cocoa, and coffee, on location. May 1935, the *Press & Journal* reported:

McKinnon's have a resident engineer at San Salvador, Central America, and since the end of the First World War, their own office at Nairobi. Their connection is world-wide wherever coffee and rice are grown. Recently they have sent mills to the Federated Malay States, the Pacific Islands, Australia, Sierra Leone.

A coffee grader by McKinnon's in use at Nairobi, Kenya. Courtesy, William McKinnon & Co Ltd.

During the second half of the twentieth century, the firm continued to concentrate on the manufacture of plantation machinery, much of their output being devoted to the production of coffee processing plant, whose various components deal with the whole complex process from de-pulping the coffee berry or cherry, fermenting the bean, washing, drying, peeling, polishing, pregrading and cylindrical grading. At Spring Garden, the

143

Wordie's horses and their carters outside McKinnon's in the 1920s, with crates of rice machinery ready for shipping to Siam (Thailand). Note the French Renaissance style extreme right. Courtesy, City of Aberdeen - Arts & Recreation Division.

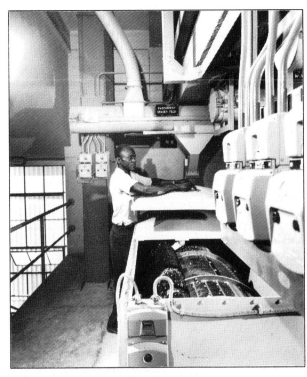

A section of McKinnon coffee machinery in use in Kenya. Courtesy, WilliamMcKinnon & Co

machinery was hand-built, turned, finished, assembled and crated for shipping. It had to be built to last, to operate smoothly in hot climates and remote areas where access was difficult and engineering skills unsophisticated.

The last David Graeme Robertson died in 1968, and was succeeded as managing director by his son, Ian Graeme, the fourth generation of Robertsons. On his retirement in 1991, McKinnon's was acquired by the firm's present managing director, Mr Sandy Cameron. He and the technical director, Mr Barry Craigmile, who started his career as an apprentice with the firm, continued to sell plant to every area of the world where coffee is grown, from Central and South America, East and West Africa, Malagasy, India, China, Thailand, Vietnam (Indo-China),

McKinnon's rice huller and polisher. Courtesy, William McKinnon & Co Ltd.

145

Malaysia, Papua New Guinea, Northern Australia.

Immediately west of the Spring Garden Iron Works, and on McKinnon property, the firm of Bell & Robertson, engineers and electricians, was set up in mid-1920s, by the Robertsons, in partnership with James Bell. They were pioneers in electrical work, and Mr Jimmy Yule, a former employee of the firm recalls that not only had the Robertsons and McKinnons intermarried, but his immediate boss was also married to a Robertson. 'Bell & Robertson and McKinnons,' he says, 'were a' throughither'. It was a useful relationship. Mackinnon's would provide foundry-made items for Bell & Robertson when required, while the latter would reciprocate with electrical equipment.

As the nineteenth century wore on, pawn brokers, chimney sweeps and spirit dealers made their businesses and homes in Windy Wynd, while Spring Garden - the name had stabilised in the singular - became increasingly industrialised with a timber yard, a coach works, the Spring Garden Mills, a confectionery works and a box factory all crowding in. Spring Garden lost some land when George Street sliced through, but compensated in 1897 by annexing Windy Wynd when the Town Council formally 'abolished' that little street. Older folk in the area, however, remember 'Windy Wynd' still being used in their youth, a name inspired by the snell north-easterly that came blasting along the street.

The Spring Garden Preserved Provision Works of Messrs Marshall & Co. was one of the early industrial arrivals in the area, customers, perhaps, for McKinnon-manufactured 'apparatus for meat preservation'. The firm was not located in Spring Garden itself, but nearby in Jopp's Lane. (One suspects another outbreak of the 'Windy Wynd' syndrome. 'Spring Garden' had much more ambience than 'Jopp's Lane'). Andrew Jopp, one of the Staats Forbes' consortium, had given his name to this narrow thoroughfare which was sandwiched between George Street and Loch Street, coming to a dead end at the back wall of Spring Garden House, as it still does. The Provision Works were on the east side. Marshall & Co flitted to handsome premises in Torry where, stubbornly continuing as the Spring Garden Works, 'they were without a rival on this side of the Atlantic ...for magnitude of operation, large-minded enterprise and high reputation'. A coachbuilding works moved into the deserted canning factory.

Back in Spring Garden proper, William Paterson & Sons, originally established around 1840 in the Gallowgate, relocated some fifty years later opposite McKinnon's Iron Works, adding the modern style, 'Manufacturing Chemist' to the older designation of 'Wholesale Druggists'. Paterson's also had a line in drysaltery items such as gums and oils, and their speciality was the manufacture of paste blacking. In the 1860s, the founder, William

Paterson, a long-serving baillie of the city, had become owner of the early nineteenth century Spring Garden House, which, surrounded by landscaped gardens, sat near the south-west corner of the street. But Paterson's occupancy of Spring Garden House was not a classic case of the master living over the shop. By the time the works had moved to Spring Garden, Paterson's grandson, Stephen, had taken over. He had already gone west to a fine new residence, 'Amatola', in Great Western Road, nowadays extended so much as a hotel that its origins as a family home are obscured. William Paterson's widow stayed on in Spring Garden House, but after her departure in the 1880s, it went over to multiple occupation, home to eight families mostly of country origin, while a warehouse was built over the gardens.

William Paterson & Sons had sizeable premises, with offices, storerooms and a large warehouse containing 'a stock of much magnitude and very large commercial value' administered by thirty clerks. The lum and archway for horse and cart access and were familiar features in the area. The firm was acquired in the mid 1920s by Mr Mitchell Ross, and his son David can recall the horse being replaced by a lorry, and the carter turned lorry driver complaining: 'The horse aye avoided the traffic, but this brute gings richt for it.'

North of Spring Garden, three new streets which linked the rival home stretches of the Inverurie turnpike, Gerrard Street, Catherine Street and Hutcheon Street were laid out early in the nineteenth century, providing a much needed contribution to Aberdeen's expansion to the north. Gerrard Street was initially described as running 'from Gallowgate to Broadford' the latter, being the original name for the section of George Street between Spring Garden and Hutcheon Street which ran through Broadford lands. Gerrard Street was feued out in 1810, partly on the old Ædipingle Croft, where King's College was the feudal superior. The name was in honour of Dr Alexander Gerard, minister of Greyfriars and Professor of Divinity at Marischal College and later at King's, having crossed to the opposition in 1776. His son Gilbert, who succeeded to his father's chair in the 1790, was dealing with applications for feus, and was well placed to advise on a choice of name. The original spelling was indeed 'Gerard', but an extra 'r' was acquired late in the nineteenth century.

Dr Alexander Gerard. A detail from John Kay's caricature 'The Seven Wise Men'. Courtesy, the University of Aberdeen.

Weavers' sheds were set up here, near the Gallowgate-head. Later in the century there would be a tallow merchant, a coach builder, and the stables of Alex Shirreffs, home to the horses of the Northern Co-operative Company (to give the Society its original title), before their Berryden stables were built.

Further north, Catherine Street and Hutcheon Street, were both described as running 'from Causewayend to Broadford'. Catherine Street, laid out partly on Tolquhoun's Croft, had opened in 1807. The ropeworks of William Routledge and his son was the best known industry here. Starting at the foot of Farquhar Place, they ran much the length of the south side of the street. Like so many Aberdeen businessmen, Routledge was a supporter of the Free Kirk movement, and it was at the ropeworks in July 1843, that a crowd of 1200, most of them ex-members of John Knox's Mounthooly, gathered and made plans to build a free church on a site across the way in Gerrard Street, backing on to the ropeworks. In Catherine Street itself, stonecutters', carters' and blacksmiths' premises would follow. A splendid photograph survives of the Vulcan Works of James Nicol, 'Mechanic and Jobbing Smith.'

The identity of Catherine remains a mystery. No puzzle about Hutcheon

The Vulcan Works of James Nicol, 'Mechanic and Jobbing Smith', Catherine Street. The mother and children (standing next to their father?) are immaculately dressed and shod.

Street, however, which was feued out in the early in the nineteenth century and named after Hugh, the proprietor of the Lands of Broadford. The widest, longest and most ambitious of these new thoroughfares, it continued, after crossing George Street, as Hutcheon Street West, through the low lying grounds of Broadford to the Lands of Gilcomston where it joined with the future Westburn Road. But Hugh Hutcheon would have had little joy of his new street. He died in 1804. Various industries were located here including Robert Davidson Snr's soap factory, the usual granite yard, and by 1909, the fully fledged Slaughter House of the Aberdeen Fleshers' Incorporation. It lay across the George Street divide, as did the rear of the mighty Broadford Works, set up in 1810 for the manufacture of linen.

Back on our own beat at the Mounthooly end of Hutcheon Street, something remarkable appeared in 1836. Our old friends John Stewart and Joseph Rowell had taken a bold step, erecting the original block of what became the Aberdeen Combworks. The scale and style of this handsome building must have set it apart from the factories of the time, many of which were little more than wooden shacks. The forty combworkers soon increased to 245 and in a few years time, the *New Statistical Account* of 1843 would be hailing Stewart & Rowell & Co, with its production rate of 43,200 combs weekly, as the largest combmaking centre in Scotland and the first to use steam power. Several prestigious journals took their cue from the *Statistical Account* and devoted substantial features on the combworks, including the Edinburgh-based *Chamber's Journal* which published a lengthy article in 1851.

The combmakers were paid a pittance in those days, but the principals, Stewart in particular, did themselves proud. One of the hallmarks of success in those days was a change of address that necessitated the purchase of a horse, even a gig, relieving one of the tedium of having to live within walking distance of one's manufactory. After a few years in the fashionable new Rosemount area, John Stewart, by 1850, was tenanting Cotton Lodge near Woodside (Primrosehill Place has been built on the site). In the 1860s he bought Craigiebuckler House, Countesswells, (from 1930, the headquarters of the Macaulay Institute). He had gone too far, however, 'overextended' himself, and had to sell up. He soon bounced back, and in 1872 was able to purchase the estate of Banchory - Banchory-Devenick, that is - on Lower Deeside.

Joseph Rowell was more of an 'over the shop' man. Though less ostentatious in his tastes than Stewart, he nevertheless had an eye for a charming residence, and was living at Maybank Cottage, Hutcheon Street West, a five minutes' walk from the combworks, by the 1830s. Joseph Rowell Snr, now simply termed 'blacksmith', had also left the West North Street area and was living round the corner from the combworks, in North

A section of the original Stewart & Rowell/Aberdeen Comb Works in Hutcheon Street, now the Duncan Centre of AMEC Offshore Developments Ltd.

Broadford as George Street then was. There he remained for many years. By 1850 the younger Rowell had moved to Rosemount, to the elegant house, View Place, (now 2a View Place and a day care centre), the view being then as now northwards to the Forbes Obelisk at Cornhill. Two years later, he was still at View Place, but as plain 'manufacturer'; 'comb' had been dropped. Before long, he had set up on his own as a 'wholesale ironmonger, manufacturer and manufacturer of nails etc.' based at 14 Upperkirkgate which was soon dignified as Ironmonger's Court. Even so, it was a far cry from the mighty combworks. He had another outlet at 16 St Paul Street and would continue in business as an ironmonger for another twenty years.

Had he quarrelled with Stewart? Perhaps as a plain technical man he may have thought Stewart was too much of a high flyer. One probably cannot blame the arrival in the business of John Stewart's son, David, for any parting of the ways. Rowell had upped sticks by the time young Stewart joined his father in 1855, after graduating MA at King's College. The firm now became Stewart, Rowell, Stewart & Co, then was abbreviated to S R Stewart & Co, but with the additional title, 'The Aberdeen Comb Works'. Expansion continued. In the 1880s, the premises had been enlarged to cover three acres with 'several large and most commodious buildings of four storeys', with warehouses, engineers' shops and 'fine private and general offices'. Over 100,000 horns arrived weekly as well as whalebone, 'vast quantities of hoofs and vulcanite', and even, on occasion, tortoiseshell, rhinoceros and buffalo horn for the manufacture of very expensive combs. Output, by a thousand workers, went up to 25 million combs in over two thousand different styles, including dog combs and mane combs. S R Stewart, it seemed, was supplying the whole world. As well as combs, horn egg spoons and egg cups, shoehorns, drinking cups, umbrella handles, paper knives, toothpicks, napkin rings, scoops, spatulas and tobacco boxes, poured forth. In addition, a fertiliser called 'Keronikon' was produced by grinding horn waste into a fine powder, much as Barry, Henry had done in years gone by.

Horn drinking mug made at Aberdeen Comb Works, circa 1940.

In 1889, *Scotland of Today* printed a lengthy and fulsome review of the firm's numerous awards and achievements hailing the Aberdeen Combworks as 'quite an ideal type of manufactory'. This may have had something to do with the fact that by then David Stewart, or Sir David as he became in 1896, was not only senior partner, but Lord Provost. In this capacity he presided over the incorporation within Aberdeen of Torry, Old Aberdeen, and Woodside where the new Stewart Park was named in his honour. In 1899, S R Stewart & Co joined forced with the Rosemount Comb Manufacturing Co in Forbes Street, (their old premises survived until the early 1990s), and G Steward & Sons of York. Thus the Aberdeen Combworks Co Ltd was born, based at Hutcheon Street.

Always in the vanguard, by the early twentieth century the firm was producing combs from 'Keronyx,' a forerunner of plastic. It was manufactured from casein, a milk by-product and supplanted horn as the chief material. Casein was inflammable, which allowed 'Keronyx' combs to hold their own against the cheap Japanese celluloid variety which were being dumped on the British market in the 1930s. Ladies who secured their tresses with the latter ran the risk of going up in flames when lighting gas ovens. 'Keronyx' combs could be manufactured in a wide range of colours, and patriotic red, white and blue combs were produced for the Silver Jubilee of King George V and Queen Mary, as *Press & Journal* reported in May 1935. It also extolled the firm's worldwide trade which included the export of 'particular smallish' combs to Africa, 'suitable for short, thick woolly hair'.

In 1937 plastic injection moulding was introduced, though I can recall a class visit to the combworks after the war when skilled women were still hand-cutting combs from horn. In 1963 Aberdeen Combworks merged with Daniel Montgomery & Sons Ltd, a Glasgow plastics firm, which moved lock, stock and barrel to Hutcheon Street. Diversification followed. Over the years, the oldest comb factory in the world, for such it was, survived a number of fires, including an inferno in 1969 which gutted the works. A year later, it rose phoenix-like out of the ashes as ACW and embarked on even wider diversification, producing bottle tops, nozzles and detonator holders in addition to traditional lines. By 1981, however, comb-making had ceased. The Tyseal Group, who since 1973 had leased the warehouse for storage, bought the buildings as their headquarters, and their founder, the late John Williams, an enthusiastic conservationist, carried out a splendid refurbishment. In the boardroom, the original 'fine, private office' which had lain neglected for many years, layers of paint and dirt were removed to reveal hand-carved pitch pine panelling, pine door-ways and a marble fireplace. An American oil-related firm, Rowan Drilling, took over this section as luxury offices. ACW Ltd moved to a modern warehouse on part of the same site to continue producing a wide range of goods by plastic injection moulding.

As well as industrial premises, there were numerous tenements in Hutcheon Street, and one of the best houses in the area, No 72, dated from the early nineteenth century. It is still known as 'the good house' among older locals because of the superior quality of the interior workmanship. A cooper, James Robertson, lived there for many years and was possibly its first owner, but by the 1890s the house had been adapted for multiple occupation and a second entrance added. Early in the twentieth century, however, it had a new lease of life as the premises of J & J Ingram, cartwrights and ploughwrights since the 1840s, when John Ingram set up in business at 34 Causewayend. Here he made stagecoaches for the Aberdeen-Inverurie route and had the satisfaction of seeing his handiwork in action, passing and repassing his workshop several times a week. In 1861 John Ingram's nephew and former apprentice also John, joined him in partnership and the firm became J & J Ingram. Two years earlier, eleven-year-old Alexander, a young brother of John Jnr, had, in turn, started his apprenticeship. In common with the McKinnons and numerous other local firms, businesses were first and foremost family businesses.

With the coming of the railways, the stagecoach trade passed, but the Ingrams diversified, making and repairing traps, carts and ploughs and had the contract for manufacturing the mail gigs. Baker's vans - horsedrawn of course - were a speciality and they made a very smart one for George

The workforce of J & J Ingram, a tough, arrogant - looking bunch who look ready to go out and conquer the world rather than just knock up a baker's van for the Co-op.

Leith the well known Ballater baker. The Ingrams would build anything in their line of business to order, from carriages to barrows. They also had a second hand department, and accepted trade-ins. In 1868, for example, they supplied a new baker's van at £40 for the Northern Co-operative Company, taking the old one as part payment.

In 1898 John Jnr 'a man of excellent business capacity' died at the age of fifty-eight. With John Snr laid to rest many years before, and with no son to succeed John Jnr, one might have expected brother Alexander, now foreman cartwright, to take the reins. But perhaps Alexander had no managerial ambitions. Whatever the reason, the firm was taken over by William Daniel, who had been a neighbour of John Ingram Jnr's in Powis Place. In a few years, the firm moved to the Hutcheon Street premises where Daniel's son young William began his apprenticeship. He recounted a memorable episode in 1911 when he and another apprentice got hold of a small boat, doubtless knocked up by the cartwrights themselves, and went for a row on the Broadford millpond on the other side of George Street. They were spotted by an enraged Broadford foreman who ran along the bank shouting and gesticulating at them.

The First World War was soon to cast its shadow and such pleasurable

The 'Good House' - No 72 Hutcheon Street

pastimes had to be put aside for the duration. Like other industrial firms around Mounthooly J & J Ingram were involved in war work, and William Daniel Jnr recalled the firm receiving a commendation for steel-ringing 163 gun carriage wheels in one day. Later, when he was at Hill 60 on the Somme, he was ordered to repair a broken wheel. He recognised it as one of J & J Ingram's, bearing his own number, 85868. Speaking of gun carriage wheels, local cart horses were enlisted during the First World War, and carried out all manner of vital haulage work on and near the front, in unpleasant and dangerous circumstances. At the end of the war, Jimmy Yule remembers, as a lad, seeing them being demobilised, coming off the wagons at the old Guild Street Goods Station. 'The Co-opie horses made off for Berryden at a quick trot, Wordie's horses for Schoolhill and Mutter Howey's for Charlotte Street. They remembered where their stables were and didn't need a second telling.'

Returning to Ingram's, some older folk have memories of enjoying genteel afternoon teas at No 72 Hutcheon Street with the grandchildren of the house around the time of the First World War.

In January 1931, Alexander Ingram retired from his position of foreman cartwright. He was eighty-three and had been with the firm for seventy-two years. He looked back on the long hours worked, often from sunrise to sunset to repair the 'equipages of the wealthy', he remembered the pneumatic tyre succeeding the rubber tyre and the coming of the motor car. William Daniel Jnr did the honours at the farewell ceremony, and Alexander's colleagues presented him with a wallet of notes and a walking stick for he had confessed that he was beginning to feel his age. It was at this time that J & J Ingram updated their designation to 'cartwrights and motorbody builders'. William Daniel Jnr subsequently took over from his father, and remained in the driving seat until the early 1960s.

Twenty years on and the old premises at No 72 Hutcheon Street, 'the good house' had become thoroughly derelict, home only to numerous pigeons. Fortunately it was then acquired by McGowan Motors, substan-

◀ The Good House No 72 Hutcheon Street.
Top left, a reconstruction by J A Sutherland
of how No 72 would have looked originally.

Centre right, by the 1980s the premises had become derelict.
Note how a second front door has appeared, indicating that the
building at some date had been divided into flats. At this point it was
home to innumerable pigeons.

Bottom left, acquired in the late 1980s by McGowan Motors,
No 72 now restored, provides office accommodation for several firms.

A lorry from the Munro's Transport fleet, one of several involved in haulage work around the Harbour area in the 1940s. As part of the war effort it has been converted from petrol to run on coal gas. Courtesy, Duncan Munro.

tially rebuilt, and now houses a number of offices and studios.

To complete our tour of the industries round about Mounthooly, mention should be made of the City Flour Mills, based in Causewayend, but backing on to the rear of the Hutcheon Street combworks. The firm flourished in the late nineteenth century and boasted a highly sophisticated processing system which produced about seven hundred sacks, or thirty five tons of flour a week. City Flour's products were sold throughout the country. Two other prominent firms in the area we have already met; R G Garvie & Sons at the foot of Canal Road, and Munro's Transport, the Mounthooly haulage company which started off in what is now Canal Place. We have come full circle.

Chapter 11

Mounthooly Memories

All roads lead to Brown's
Notice outside A G Brown Grocer, 212 Gallowgate

Mounthooly with its large population and its numerous industrial and commercial enterprises, all concentrated in a relatively small area, was one of the busiest, most lively places in Aberdeen. Each tenement was virtually a community in itself. Some were home to as many as fifty children, perfectly feasible where there were six houses (flats) or more in a tenement. Children were everywhere, going back and forward to school, morning and afternoon, or playing in the streets. Before school, they might be out delivering milk or bread, but the eight o'clock hooter, announcing the start of another day in the granite yards, engineering works and mills, was the signal for those bairns still abed to get up and get ready for school. Joan Gray whose home at No 15 Canal Street was directly opposite the back of the school could stroll across at the last minute. The only drawback was that the railway lay in her path, so a surreptitious crossing was called for. Care had to be taken not to be mown down by the goods wagons which ran regularly down the line to Waterloo at that time. She had picked up this bad habit from her father, an engine driver, who used to walk up the line to start work at Kittybrewster, but the family was not supposed to follow his example. One day during the war, Joan was sent home to collect a forgotten gas mask. Her teacher, amazed that she could have made the long haul

Crossing the Waterloo line was a short cut to school. The railway line was laid out in the bed of the Aberdeenshire Canal. The Mounthooly Newsagent, formerly Barry's Cafe is seen on the left.

along Causewayend, Mounthooly and Canal Street and back in such a short space of time, never 'twigged' about the covert use of the railway line.

Later on in the day, the workforce from Barry, Henry, and John M Henderson's, from Munro's Transport, and R G Garvie would converge on Barry's Cafe at their breaktime. Mounthooly housewives made trips to the local shops and the dairy twice, even three times a day. The amount of storage space offered by the kitchen press was limited and refrigerators were unheard of.

The shops around Mounthooly, Mr Tommy Donaldson recalls, were at the very heart of the community. Room at home was limited, but the shops provided a meeting-place where adults could exchange gossip, and a base round which the children could organise their street games. Tommy Donaldson remembers Brown the Grocer at the foot of the Gallowgate, across from Adam and Craigmile. A board outside the shop proclaimed, 'All Roads lead to Brown's,' and there was a map to prove it. 'Broonie's had everything,' recalls Joan Gray. Their bottled beer is well-remembered. Several families lived in the 'houses' or flats above the shop which was built on the wedge-shaped corner of the Gallowgate and the cobbles that carried round to West North Street were slippery with age. Near to Brown's on the West North Street side was Wood's cooked meat shop which sold tripe - and pig's trotters. These were skewered on a knitting needle and eaten as a great

Brown's window display advertising bottled beer and whisky. Note the price.

treat of a Saturday night. Next door, Mr Brown's son had the shoemaker's shop. Coletta's chip shop was next door, and Scullion's fish shop was across on the Nelson Street corner.

Round on the Gallowgate side of Brown's, was Shand, the chemist's that everyone went to. Further up, William Kitson had succeeded Samuel Willans at the old Porthill Factory as early as 1865. His line of business was the same, though initially he operated as a rag and bone man as well as a stoneware merchant. The entrance was via Seamount Place as in the old days. There was also access from West North Street by a flight of stairs, as long and steep as those between Bridge Street and Crown Terrace, but extremely narrow. There was little room to pass, and no room at all if you met anyone carrying a wide load. William Kitson lived over the shop, at No 1 Seamount Place, but by the end of the nineteenth century his successor, George E Kitson had moved to No 7 King's Crescent, almost opposite Samuel Willans' old home at Friendly Bank. His job description too, was more 'upmarket' than that of his forebear, a glass and china, rather than stoneware merchant. Across Seamount Place from Kitson's in the 1920s, was an electrician and electro-plater, the Gallowgate's own inventor, who had devised an electric hot bottle consisting of an aluminium flask filled

This 1958 photograph of Mounthooly prior to demolition makes an interesting comparison with virtually the same scene on page 32. The post office is still in business but next door, Mitchell & Muil's is boarded up. In front of the church, Adam & Craigmile and A & A Douglas have already gone. In the distance, at right angles, is 'Mount Pleasant', the first house in Canal Street, with its arch to the right. The Northern Co-operative shops are visible extreme left, and beyond, the start of Causewayend can be glimpsed, with the telephone of the 'Bobbies' Boxie' on the pavement. Of all the buildings shown, only the church and the furthest cottage in Mounthooly, formerly Barry's Cafe and now the Mounthooly Newsagent, remain. Courtesy, Aberdeen Journals Ltd.

with brick dust into which an electric cable was inserted. The power was turned on for a time, then the heated flask placed in the bed. Further up, nearer the Gallowgate, or the Porthill Church as it was sometimes called, was a branch of the Mascot dress shop.

Across from Brown's was Mrs Greig's Sweetie Shop, famous for its toffee and boiled sweets, made on the premises. Round toffee stamps and coconut chips were very popular, and quarter of a pound cost three farthings. The shop had a double frontage and Muriel Slessor remembers two windows being filled with sweets, with never a repetition of colours. Next door to Greig's, virtually at the foot of the Gallowgate, was the Northern Co-op's Gallowgate-head Branch. A grocer's, butcher's and baker's opened at Nos 217-218a in 1880 the Co-opie's seventh branch. Writing in the *Evening Express* in November 1991, George Tait remembered the scene sixty years earlier:

The grocer's was particularly busy, packed to the doors on an Thursday evening, the day when most working people were paid. No self-service supermarkets then; simply a row of shop assistants standing virtually shoulder to shoulder, dealing with the crush of customers clutching their weekly shopping lists.

Ben Cormack, the undertaker, after moving from Mounthooly, had gone into the last building in the Gallowgate, No 219 on the other side of Farquhar Place from the Co-op. This was a small, dark funeral parlour, and he also lived over the shop. Next door, at No 1 Causewayend was Pawn Bob's or 'The Ramer', more correctly the Equitable Loan Co, 'a helpmeet for the many poor people living in the area,' recalled Mr Tait. There was a newsagent's, and a butcher's, Sutherland's, later, G M Lyon's. Long ago, Isaac Benzie had one of his drapery branches hereabouts and sold his own make of stockings. 'I had a fawn pair,' recalls Muriel Slessor, 'and I still remember the day when a couple of loons cried "marless stockings" at my friend and me. I thought it was my Isaac Benzie's stockings that didn't match, but it was my friend that had the odd pair.'

The Stag's Head pub, 'the Beastie', was at the Hutcheon Street corner, on the ground floor of a four-storey tenement, one of the tallest buildings in the territory. It had a public bar and a snug. Licensees over the years included Mrs John Miller and R M Milne. The last owners were the brewers Tennent Caledonian.

Across the Hutcheon Street junction was Carcone's 'Gold Medal' ice-cream parlour, one of the older buildings in Causewayend, attractively

Carcone's shop on the corner of Hutcheon Street and Causewayend. Courtesy, City of Aberdeen - Planning Division.

rounded to take advantage of the corner site. Today Carcone's premises are no great distance away in Nelson Street. A number of Italians who came to Aberdeen in the late nineteenth and early twentieth centuries made their mark as purveyors of ice cream and fish and chips around Mounthooly. We have already met a few; Canale, Coletta, d'Alessandro. The father of the celebrated painter, Alberto Morocco, sold ice-cream from a barrow before buying a shop in Causewayend opposite the school. Muriel Slessor remembers the Morocco family, and their bright wee house where there were always flowers in the win-

Alberto Morocco. Self- portrait.

dow. Guiseppe Nardi's chipper was at the corner of Berry Street and the Gallowgate, and although his chips were fine, Anne Brand remembers her mother warning her against buying chips there. Nardi was suspected of flicking his cigarette ash into the fryer.

Back in Causewayend, Muriel Slessor has pleasant memories of Candy Jean's shop, beyond the Morocco's, at No 43, opposite Canal Road. Never seen without her apron, Jean lived and worked there, making candy and chocolate nuggets in two colours. It was a welcoming place. The zinc counter with its brass edging was spotless and there was always a fire with a cat sitting in front of it on a clootie rug. Jeannie Robertson, the well known folk-singer lived nearby, at No 45 Causewayend.

On the other side of the road, back at the junction with Mounthooly was the stretch of Causewayend that lay on the old lands of Tolquhoun's Croft. It started at the 'Bobbies' Boxie', the police sub-station, set back and rather hidden by the Mounthooly post office which jutted out. Walter Michie owned the whole tenement building, Nos 6 - 10, next to the Bobbies' Boxie and had his large grocer's shop on the ground floor. Then came the White Rose chip shop run by the Carcones who, like Walter Michie, owned their whole tenement, Nos 12-16. Jappy's was next door, a tiny shop that sold everything and was much frequented by Cassie-end scholars before starting their day's studies. James Douglas, general merchant, was at No 18, and past the little pend leading into Causey Place was Nos 24-28. This was the property that we left in 1807 in Chapter Two, in the hands of the Narrow Wynd Society. The Society rouped it in 1858 to a George Street hairdresser, Charles Cockerill, for £147. It was then acquired by a local property owner, Miss Jemima Fowlie, who later sold it to Robert Simpson Jessamine. His son

Robert Bendelow Jessamine sold it to Forbes Wright who like Ben Cormack had moved down from Mounthooly, and was thus the second hairdresser to have a shop here.

The Jessamines also owned Bendelow's pie shop, a little further along, next to Causewayend School, where the pupils used to queue up at the hatch during break. Bendelow's Pies were legendary not just around Mounthooly, but throughout Aberdeen. A week-end treat was a 'carry out' of hot meat pies. Anyone wanting gravy had to take along a plate. A particular Saturday favourite was an apple bannock, which could be ordered large enough feed a family of six. The purchaser brought along a cloth to wrap it in. People still remember rhymes about Bendelow's - Who's got eyes like Bendelow's pies?' Isobel Donaldson recalls - or argue over the merits of their pastry. 'Mother was a good pastry-maker, and she felt Bendelow's pastry was too white,' says Muriel Slessor. Jimmy Yule remembers being in the Nelson Street 'Globie' one memorable evening during the silent era. 'In those days a man behind the screen invented the dialogue to suit the action of the film being shown,' he recollects. 'In one scene a grand lady entered her carriage and the voice behind the screen gave the order to the coachman: "James, drive me round to Bendelow's." That brought the house down.' The Jessamine family also distinguished themselves in other walks of life with a well known local doctor and dentist in their ranks.

Further along, where the Brown & Root offices now stand at the foot of Izzie Masson's Brae, was a little shop that sold everything. Norah Morrison recalls a tall lady with a black velvet band round her neck. 'The shop was always very clean, with a cloth over the corned beef.'

Children were always on hand to run errands for folk unable to get to the shops. Mrs Walker (nee Fyfe) who has lived in the Mounthooly area all her life, remembers her mother persuading her to run errands to Paper Annie's for an elderly neighbour, Fanny Craig. The little girl was a bit unsure of Fanny because her nose was brown - but that was only because the old lady enjoyed a pinch of snuff. Mrs Walker still remembers Annie (Edgar?) carefully weighing out tuppence worth and wrapping it in a yellow twist of paper. Alex Slessor used to deliver bread as a boy and he had customers up the close at the Powis Barracks. 'They were cheery folk, and they ordered so many plain loaves - bigger than you get today - that they had to bring down huge pillow cases to carry them in. In the west end you'd carry in a tray with maybe just a loaf or a cake on it.'

For social life, there was, of course, the popular 'Globie', entrance 1d, which drew its patrons from College Bounds and the Spital as well as the

Gallowgate and the Mounthooly area. Tommy Donaldson remembers the hard wooden benches, with everyone squeezing along to make room for others. The numerous churches in the area were also social centres under whose banner a whole range of activities were on offer. Norah Morrison recalls attending the Band of Hope at the Gallowgate Kirk, and the IOGT Temperance League in Seamount Place. There was also a mission in Justice Street. She also had her music lessons, and from the late 1930s, there was St Catherine's Club for Girls in West North Street. (St K's has been replaced by 'The Lemon Tree' which offers food, drink and entertainment, but the building remains). A walk or a tram ride along George Street took you into town. The fare to the Queen in St Nicholas Street was 1d from the Fraser Place stop, and you could watch the horses being shod in the smithy nearby as you waited. Or you could walk in as far as Hutcheon Street and save a halfpenny. 'It was,' says Norah Morrison, 'a good childhood.'

Accommodation ranged from the primitive to the better class. There were groups of tenement houses that were considered very poor, some in Causey Place off Causewayend, in Causewayend itself, in Berry Street, in Gerrard Street and West North Street, on the south side of Hutcheon Street. Overcrowding was taken as a fact of life, as were bedrooms without doors, rickety stairs and a shared cold water tap on each floor - though one family who lived above a baker's suddenly found they had hot water after some

Gerrard Street in the early 1960s, looking west towards George Street. The tenements on both sides of John Knox church await demolition. Courtesy, Aberdeen Journals Ltd.

improvements were carried out at the shop below. Out the back would be the washhouse, the cellars, the green and a couple of shared lavvies. But former locals will tell you: 'We didn't know we were hard up. Nobody told us we were "deprived". And we kept an eye on the elderly and folk who were really up against it.'

There were those who weren't too badly off. The 1891 census returns, for example, reveal some large families with the father and several sons and daughters all in employment. The young people would contribute to the household budget, and folk in the district were great savers. Although there were already three rival banks in the area, in 1903, the Aberdeen Savings Bank opened its first full-time branch in rented property at No 411 George Street, near the junction with Hutcheon Street. It became so busy that the trustees decided that a new, custom-built bank was justified. They purchased a site opposite Catherine Street, and by 1908, their architect Dr William Kelly had produced a splendid new bank disguised as wee Greek temple. And so it remains.

Those with modest savings may have contemplated a move to a better class of tenement, or even a flat in one of the two-flatted houses that went up in Sunnybank in the 1920s. By the 1930s it was possible to buy a two-bedroomed house for well under £500. After a down payment of around £40, weekly repayments often worked out less than the rent of a tenement house. Using the excellent transport system or owning a bike did away with the necessity to live near the workplace.

But many others had neither the means nor the desire to make the move from Mounthooly and its cheery comradeship. The Brand family of Canal Street are recalled with particular affection. 'Mrs Brand was a gem,' say Joan Gray. 'She had so much time for all the children.' Anne and Laura sang at John Knox's, in concerts, and had their secondary schooling at the Central before starting their professional singing career, but never forgot their roots. 'At the Middle School reunions,' says Joan Gray, everyone talks about what a friendly place it was around Mounthooly. Many old pupils have done very well in their adult life, but still look back to their schooldays at Causewayend and the Middle as the happiest of days.'

'Folk were really proud of their houses,' recalls Alex Slessor. 'In Causewayend they would colour their doorsteps maybe ochre or pink or green or yellow. They would sit of a summer evening on the doorsteps chatting. It was a real village atmosphere.'

It took Sir Henry Alexander and Hitler to change all that.

Part Five

The Coming of the Roundabout

Canal Street Mounthooly

After the raid of April, 1943, survivors in Charles Street search for their belongings amidst the rubble.

Chapter 12

War and Devastation

Nearly whole streets have been removed in conformity with the plans for large development schemes.

A Thousand Years of Aberdeen, Alexander Keith, 1972

The area suffered during the war. 'Soapy' Ogston's and the neighbouring McBride's Bar in Loch Street were blitzed on February 13, 1941, leaving seventeen killed. In April 1942, John M Henderson's King Street works was bombed and Seamount Place and the Porthill Church in the Gallowgate, were damaged in the same attack. The worst raid was carried out by Dornier 217 bombers flying in from Stavanger on 21 April 1943. Thirty-one tons of bombs fell on Aberdeen that day, with casualities of ninety-seven killed, 235 injured, though the final figures are still uncertain. 'Working Class Area Suffers Badly,' the *Evening Express* reported the following day. Aberdeen Harbour, apparently, was the objective, but the Dorniers flew low along the line of George Street, bombing the streets around. Causewayend Church was badly damaged as we know. The slaughterhouse in Hutcheon Street, Fraser Place, Catherine Street, Elmbank Road and Maberly Street all suffered direct hits. Charles Street linking George Street and Causewayend just north of Fraser Place was blitzed, and one house was completely taken out, killing everyone inside.

Some unusual 'howfs' did duty as air-raid shelters, including the basement of Barry's Cafe at No 29 Mounthooly where the fireplaces were still intact. This shop is now a newsagent's and one customer, a lady in her eighties who was born there, remembers that a fire would be kindled during air-raids to make the 'shelter' cosy.

The local engineering firms contributed magnificently to the war effort. The bombing of John M Henderson's works in 1942 did not discourage the firm from producing a wide range of equipment including 5.5 inch gun howitzer carriages, which presented a formidable array as they lay awaiting transport in the King's Works assembly bay. Ammunition hoists, antisubmarine devices, jacks for bombers, mine sweeping and aircraft carrier parts, Bailey bridge and Churchill tank parts and much more was produced. The bland description: 'five aerial cableways for a large British Naval Base', was a reference to the building of famous Churchill barriers, no less. After the defences of Scapa Flow in the Orkneys were breached by the U-47 in 1939 and the Royal Oak torpedoed, the barriers - great blocks of concrete linking five islands - were constructed to block off the eastern approaches to Scapa. Aerial cableways were urgently required to transport building materials, so five blondins built by Henderson's for the Middle East, probably the very ones that were used for the Nile barrage, were brought home, re-erected and pressed into service in the Orkneys. After the war, Henderson's were able to capitalise on experience gained for example in the manufacture of mechanical handing plant. McKinnon's too, switched its resources for the duration. They produced formidable quantities of munitions, heavy explosives, baffle plates, areo engine parts and much more. An area at the west end of their premises was cleared, converted into a shooting range and used by the Home Guard.

The devastation wrought during the war continued for years after, but at the behest of the local authority, rather than Hitler. The scale was far greater, but the cause was worthy. Back in 1933, the Aberdeen and District Joint Town Planning Scheme, masterminded by Lord Provost Sir Henry Alexander, and hailed as a model of its kind, had identified the city's densely populated zones including the Gallowgate and Causewayend-Mounthooly areas. The march of progress dictated the demolition of worn out, insanitary property and the rehousing of displaced residents in the new council housing schemes .

As early as 1935, the property at Nos 2-4 Mounthooly and Nos 192-194 West North Street, owned by Antonio d'Alessandro and his wife, had been bought by Aberdeen Council at the beginning of a drive to redevelop the area. Plans had gone on the back burner during the war, but the publication in 1952 of the Council commissioned report, *Granite City: A Plan for Aberdeen* by W Dobson Chapman and Charles F Riley, signalled recommencement of activity. It was estimated that over 8000 families were living in crowded conditions in Aberdeen, and the City Development Plan of 1949 published in *Granite City* showed the old Gallowgate-head area and beyond highlighted 'with a view to carrying out the maximum possible clearance and redevelopment'.

Acquisition of properties recommenced and continued apace. The row of old Mounthooly tenements, featured in our photographs, were purchased from Dr John Wight's trustees in 1951. Demolition at the 'John Knox's' cluster of shops had begun by 1958. They were replaced by a grassy patch and a seat. Across the way, the quaint old tenement at Nos 1-3 Mounthooly and its neighbour with the chubby dormers, No 5-7, were razed to the ground. Mrs Jean Mackay at No 1 Mounthooly had already moved the sub-post office across to No 3 Causewayend adjoining No 5a where John and Grace McIntosh had been newsagents since 1949. (After Mrs Mackay's death, John McIntosh took over as sub-postmaster). The site where these quaint tenements had stood for so long was now landscaped with grass and garden seats, and in 1960 a normal-sized roundabout appeared at Mounthooly. John Junor, keeping a step ahead of the demolitions, had moved from No 7 to take over the grocer's and newsagents at No 13a Mounthooly. Gambling from licensed premises was now legal, and in June, 1961, the Council granted him permission to convert part of a dwelling house at No 13 for use as a betting office, but only until 1966 when the remaining tenements were due for demolition. Round in Causewayend, the properties of Robert Jessamine, Joseph Carcone, Walter Michie and Forbes Wright had all been acquired by Aberdeen Council by 1962. The following year, R G Garvie & Sons requested first refusal of any ground that might become available as the result of the dualling of Causewayend and the consequent realignment of Canal Road, but at that time, the council was unable to commit itself.

West North Street was dualled in 1966, and by 1970, the council's comprehensive development scheme, involving the George Street, Hutcheon Street, Mounthooly, Gallowgate and Spring Garden area was in full swing. Redevelopment of the area and the road improvement scheme were concurrent and it is now hard to say exactly what came down because it was in the way of the latter, and what was demolished because it was deemed 'unfit for human habitation'. Causewayend became a dual carriageway in 1972, while the construction of a new two-and-a-half acre roundabout covering the site of the old Gallowgate-head took place. Among buildings that had to go to accommodate the roundabout were those in the streets radiating from the old Gallowgate-head, including all properties between

171

The Mounthooly area in 1966. Demolition is underway, with Brown's at the foot of the Gallowgate gone. Left, the Northern Co-operative buildings and Greig's sweetie shop next door still stand. On the right is the former Nelson Street UP Church, alias the 'Globie' with the box accommodating the talkie speakers, added in 1930, still visible at the rear. It was subsequently refurbished by Mr Ean Emslie. The little shops below John Knox's Church have been replaced by a landscaped area, and another north of the small roundabout has replaced the two oldest tenements. The gaunt tenements that used to adjoin them survive, and behind them are the premises where Munro's Transport started off, occupying what was once the long gardens of the 'genteel' houses of the cul-de-sac, which are still visible. Just across the railway line, Canal Street remains in its original state. The row of shops beside Causewayend School are already roofless - the awnings belong to Walter Michie, the grocer. Courtesy, Aberdeen Journals Ltd.

172

The shops beside Causewayend School, built on what was once Tolquhoun's Croft have gone. Centre, one of the 'genteel' houses in the Canal Place cul-de-sac awaits demolition. Courtesy, City of Aberdeen - Planning Division.

Mounthooly and Causewayend School. The *Aberdeen Pub Companion* included a requiem for the local pub:

> The Stag's Head which served a vast tenement area (now mostly demolished), has disappeared into a welter of mud, shored-up buildings and uncompleted roadworks, although we are told that this morass will eventually become the huge Mounthooly roundabout, a stage in the city's inner ring-road system. In October 21, 1971, it finally closed its doors, and the actual stag's head is now in the hallway of the Park Hotel Macduff.

The Stag's Head finally came down in May 1972.

It took seven years to build the roundabout, from 1970 until 1977, and if that seems an unconscionably long time even for such a monster, it was partly because of delays occasioned by finding alternative sites for firms on the demolition path, and dealing with objectors. Among the latter was Mckinnon's Spring Garden Iron Works and Aberdeen Lads Club whose Gallowgate premises had been demolished only a few years earlier. They thought they would be safe in Hutcheon Street, only to find themselves marooned high and dry on the roundabout. The problem was resolved

This 1972 photograph of virtually the same site as the one on page 172, shows how far demolition has progressed. The Stag's Head pub was located in the tall building across from Causewayend School. Courtesy, Aberdeen Journals Ltd.

The gables of the Comb Works can be seen across Hutcheon Street through the gap created by the demolition of the Aberdeen Lads Club. Courtesy, City of Aberdeen - Planning Division.

when they moved to Woodside. Mackinnon's stayed firm, however, and after a public inquiry, the Secretary of State's decreed that the company would not be required to move from Spring Garden for at least fifteen years.

The demolition of the Spring Garden Iron Works in the early 1990s provided an unusual view of the Gerrard Street Baptist Church (formerly John Knox).

175

In fact it was twenty. It must have been a considerable relief to the Council that these difficulties were resolved by March 1972, for a year earlier, grant aid, which amounted to 75% of project costs, was suspended by the Scottish Office until such time as problems were resolved.

By 1975, the last shop lying in the path of the roundabout, the McIntosh's newsagent's, and sub-post office in Causewayend was awaiting demolition. Back in 1970, the McIntoshes, with an eye to the future, had acquired Barry's Cafe at 29 Mounthooly. Most of the engineering firms whose workforce had once patronised the cafe were now gone, and the McIntoshes now set about transforming it into a newsagent's. This building alone remains of the old 'front row' on the west side of Mounthooly and Mr Alan Anderson, newsagent there since 1987, still gets his electricity bills addressed to Barry's Cafe.

Chapter 13

A Glance up the Gallowgate

The street is a shambles and irretrievable.
A Thousand Years of Aberdeen, Alexander Keith, 1972

Even before Mounthooly and the area around was razed to the ground, redevelopment was well underway in the Gallowgate, a spate of demolitions had made a clean sweep of the old Porthill near its junction with Mounthooly. This perhaps is the place to have a brief glance at this ancient road whose fate has not been a happy one. Along with Broad Street it was once Aberdeen's principal thoroughfare, where the wealthy had their mansions set in spacious feus, with 'tails' or long gardens, sloping down to the Lochside on the west or the Back Causeway on the east. As the nineteenth century progressed, the well-to-do moved to more fashionable parts of town and the Gallowgate became notoriously rundown. Unfortunately, the old mansions contained within themselves the seeds of their own destruction. With little or no local authority control, and lacking the clear definition of the 'houses' of a custom-built tenement, these handsome dwellings, once they went over to multiple tenancy, became virtual rookeries, their very spaciousness encouraging subdivision upon subdivision. And to provide for a burgeoning population, their gardens, orchards and forecourts were built over with back houses and fore houses.

The sixteenth century L-shaped Mar's Castle, with its double corbel course and red pantiles, traditionally the town house of one of the Earls of Mar, was a case in point. (It was almost the spitting image of Provost Ross's

The Gallowgate showing Mar's Castle, with its double corbel course, red pantiles and corbelled-out stair turret. The rear of one of Bain's horse buses, which operated on the Marywell Street-Old Aberdeen route between the 1860s and 1870s, can be seen heading towards Broad Street.

House in the Shiprow, which itself evaded demolition by the narrowest squeak, and now houses Aberdeen's Maritime Museum). Described by the architectural historian Edward Meldrum, as 'an excellent example of a mediaeval townhouse', Mar's Castle stood on the east side of the Porthill, within the port, almost opposite Innes Street with its own close, garden and summer house. By 1886, however, A M Munro, city chamberlain and historian noted that 'almost every foot of the garden is now occupied with houses scattered about in picturesque confusion'. In 1897, the dilapidated Castle was acquired by the Town Council and pulled down, its erstwhile residents presumably decanted into less insalubrious dwellings. The official reason for demolition was that the building was unsafe and unfit for human habitation. So, I dare say, was Broadford's disused brick warehouse, which, as I write a century later, has been converted into luxury flats.

Sir William Geddes knew the Gallowgate intimately when it was rundown though still intact. He argued that 'if handled imaginatively, it could be made as romantic and picturesque as Edinburgh's High Street'. The words of the formidable 'Homer' Geddes, Professor of Greek, then Principal of Aberdeen University during the era from 1855 until 1900, and a man before his time, fell on deaf ears. No positive future, no policy worthy of the ancient route seems to have been considered. At that time, 'it's aul, pull it doon,' was the watchword. It was not then appreciated that the restoration of those Gallowgate buildings worth retaining could have gone hand-in-hand with improved housing conditions. And to be fair, the building and restoring techniques available to the modern conservationist were then undreamed of.

A piecemeal demolition in the name of slum clearance and road widening gathered pace in the 1900s when much of the east side, with its seventeenth and eighteenth century houses and closes was cleared away. Moving towards Broad Street, the very fine mansion of Gilbert Gerard, advocate, built in 1787 and later a girls' hospital, hence the name of its close, Hospital Court, was pulled down in 1905. The site appears to have lain empty until the post war era when the Ministry of Public Building and Works, which at that time had *carte blanche* to erect hideous structures the length and breadth of the country, built Greyfriars House, hailed as the ugliest office block in Aberdeen.

Returning to the Porthill, the Quakers had a presence there for two hundred years. In the 1660s they acquired ground adjacent to the south wall of the garden of Mar's Castle to use as a burying ground. One story suggests that they came there because they were denied the right of interment in consecrated ground. Another, quite the reverse, insists that the Quakers had certain objections to being buried in the town's kirkyard of St Nicholas. The magistrates, annoyed at what seemed a ploy to evade burial fees, insisted that they return the graveyard to its former use (as a kailyard), exhume their dead and re-inter them in St Nicholas Churchyard where burial dues could be exacted. Whatever the truth, the Quakers were undeniably subject to persecution in Aberdeen in the seventeenth century and the great stone dykes which enclosed the graveyard 'were again and again demolished by order of the Town Council', according to Alexander Gammie.

In 1827 the Quakers, still persevering at the Porthill, built a plain, solid Meeting House beside their burying ground. It served this quiet and peace-loving community for over forty years. It was built says Alexander Gammie:

on one of the most elevated sites in Aberdeen, the ground rising in a steep gradient from the highest point in the Gallowgate. The building was a very substantial one, the walls being of a considerable thickness. Latterly it was used for many years as a currying shop by Messrs John Watt & Son, leather merchants. Under the Gallowgate Improvement Scheme of it 1907 it was swept away.

Presumably the walls of the graveyard, if still standing, were dinged

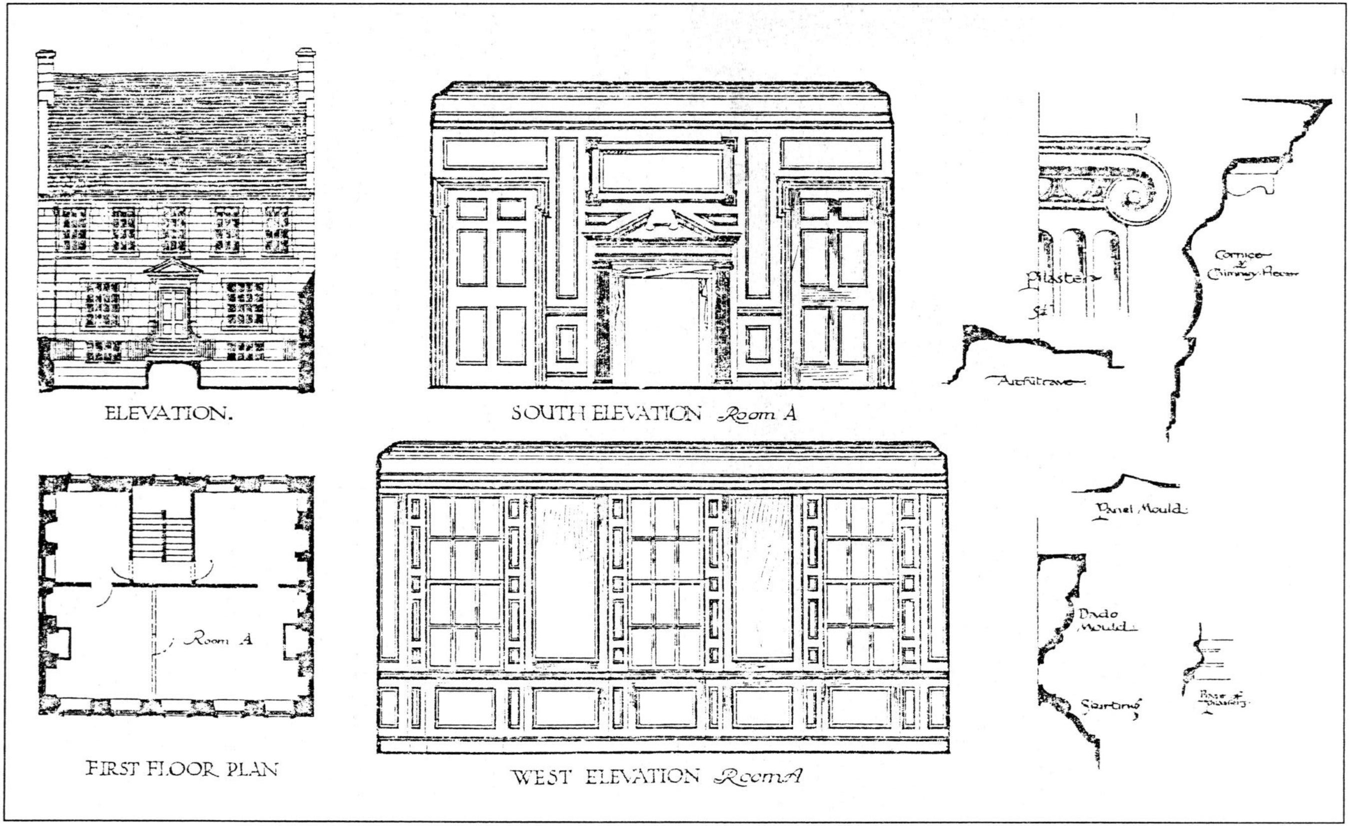

Cornice & Chimney-Piece

Panel Mould

Dado Mould

Base of Skirting

Skirting

Pilaster Sill

Architrave

SOUTH ELEVATION. *Room A*

WEST ELEVATION. *Room A*

ELEVATION.

FIRST FLOOR PLAN

Room A

Details of Gilbert Gerard's mansion in the Gallowgate.

180

The Gallowgate around 1930, looking towards Mounthooly (and reminiscent of College Bounds). The tall Co-op buildings can be seen at the foot of the road. Note the handsome lamppost, left and Nardi's chipper half way down. There is an interesting selection of forms of transport.

doon at the same time.

Demolition continued during the 1920s, and in 1936, Tommy Scott Sutherland, councillor for Ruthrieston ward and housing convener toured the Gallowgate area with fellow councillors to see at first hand the deplorable conditions still prevailing in the surviving slums; nine of a family to a room; eight families sharing a single lavatory. Tommy certainly could not be accused of not having a policy; as a highly successful architect it was usually to demolish and rebuild, and the type of rebuilding that he envisaged at the Porthill was blocks of four storey flats at right angles to the street, with the open spaces between each block laid out as playgrounds or gardens.

The war called a halt to such plans. Bob Gibb, writing in *Leopard Magazine* in March 1995, looking back to his days as a butcher's delivery boy fifty years earlier, caught the flavour of the old Gallowgate before it vanished completely:

The Gallowgate of these days was alive. Age-blackened granite tenements crowded their way up the hill. Shops of all descriptions did a roaring trade despite the presence of the Co-opie Arcade at the other end. Those tenements were literally warrens with long lobbies stretching way back, hiding room after room of crowded families. It was the smell I remember most vividly - cats ... Added to that was the all-pervading dampness, and ancient, thick, bottle-green oil paper hanging off the walls. But happy they were, these people.

The Gallowgate shops were as famous as those of Mounthooly and the shopkeepers enjoyed their daily claik with Sir George Adam Smith, Principal of Aberdeen University from 1910-36 and one of the city's great men, on his walk from Chanonry Lodge to Marischal College.

A poem was written in their honour by Isabella Miller who was born in 1882 and remembered them all.

> *There was Geordie Mundie and Johnny Ramsay,*
> *Wi stockit shops of haberdashery.*
> *And Annie Edgar supplied your paper,*
> *Next door to her was Crolly the baker.*
>
> *There was Kitson's rag store further up,*
> *For a handful o rags he gied you a cup.*
> *And old Mrs McIntyre wha mended your gamp,*
> *And the three brass balls beside the lamp.*
>
> *There was Tucker the butcher wha sellt cheap beef*
> *For some old bread you got sausage meat.*
> *There was Dr McRobbie in next door.*
> *His senna leaves fair gared you roar. . .*
>
> *At the top of Windy Wynd, Jose Wilson's shop*
> *Sold anything from a tiara to a top*
> *And Diack's coal store round the corner*
> *Wi paraffin, sticks and coals to order*
>
> *There was Porthill and the Middle School*
> *Where the Heidie knew the way to rule.*
>
> *There was Drunken Toughie and Cackie Eppie*
> *Barrel Doddie and Cabin Jessie. . .*
> *There was Hackett Beef and Fish Neddy*
> *Currant Bun and Fartin Meggie*

The Gallowgate shopkeepers enjoyed a touch of internationalism. They included in their number, a Russian grocer with an unpronounceable

182

name who sold paraffin, onions and firelighters, and a German, Mr Castol, who sold fruit from a barrow at the corner of St Paul Street .

After the passing of the Town and Country Planning Act of 1947 there was an attempt to list the Gallowgate's remaining historic buildings but to little avail. By the early 1960s, the pre-war schemes had gathered steam again, and what remained of the Porthill was razed to the ground. Kitson's glass and china warehouse - the old Porthill Factory - and its neighbours came down including, Aberdeen Lads Club and the Gallowgate Church which had survived the blitz of April, 1942, in vain. The council housing which took their place was roughly as envisaged by Tommy Sutherland, with the addition of two high rise flats, Seamount and Porthill Courts. The result was a collection of four-storey boxes (some built over the old Quaker meeting house and burying ground), flanking two very tall boxes, and the whole set off by the West North Street car park; not so much a concrete jungle as a concrete jumble. On the west side, the demolitions of 1963

The easterly slopes of the Porthill, now a concrete jumble. Porthill and Seamount Courts loom above the West North Street car park and dominate the skyline.

included No 173 Gallowgate, on the Young Street corner. It would have stood just outside the port. It was, wrote Edward Meldrum:

for long the oldest remaining house in the street, being early 18th century in date. Gable-end to the street, it was built of 'heathen' granite boulders with a flat arched pend leading to an inner court and having forestairs giving access from the side lane to the upper floor.

183

The Aberdeen College, formerly Aberdeen Technical College occupies the site of Young Street and Berry Street.

The whole of Young Street and Berry Street vanished at this time, replaced by the Aberdeen Technical College, a new and upgraded version of the Trades College in George Street. Straddling across to the old Lochside, the new College was another variation on the box theme. D Macandrew & Co Ltd departed to Ferryhill in the 1960s, where the firm continued to trade in Oldmill Road off Bon-Accord Street for a time. Innes Street held out for some years, and though it eventually went, a narrow right of way currently provides access between the Gallowgate and Loch Street.

At the very time demolition and reconstruction was taking place in the Porthill, 'slum' property in Old Aberdeen, worn out cottages and tenements in College Bounds and the High Street, many coeval with, and in no better shape than those in the Gallowgate, were being faithfully restored by Aberdeen University. The result of this far-seeing enterprise was one of the most effective and outstanding restorations in post-war Britain which brought architects of international standing flocking to the Aulton. Had a similar policy been followed in the Gallowgate, Aberdeen would have had a unique Royal Mile - and a half. What is surprising is that the two schemes, one destroying a vital part of the local heritage, the other preserving and enhancing it, were carried out under the same planning authority - though under the aegis of different corporate landlords - almost within a stone's

The listed buildings are to the left of the Co-op buildings. All were demolished.

throw of each other on the same ancient highway north.

Demolition at the south end of the Gallowgate took place in the late 1980s when a number of buildings, by then listed as being of considerable historic interest, were pulled down to clear ground for the proposed Bredero-Aberdeen District Council redevelopment of the area. Among them were Nos 47 and Nos 49-51, the former late eighteenth, the latter early nineteenth century, both B-listed; Nos 53-57 and Nos 59-63, both eighteenth century and B-listed. The former group included the fine pend archway which led through to Chapel Court; in the court itself, the eighteenth century C-listed manse to St Paul's Episcopal Chapel also went. (The Chapel itself had been demolished in 1865 and replaced by St Paul's Episcopal Church, entered by Loch Street). At Nos 65-75, the Northern Co-operative's Gallowgate frontage, built in 1867, was also pulled down, along with the rest of the famous Loch Street headquarters, a much regretted demolition. It had been preceded by that of the neighbouring St Paul's Episcopal Church. Fortunately the modern residential and office accommodation which has replaced this unique Gallowgate group is well-suited to the existing townscape.

The early eighteenth century gateway was reassembled in Loch Street where it sits in limbo. More aptly, it might serve as the gateway to the nearby new and attractive townhouses of Candlemakers' Court. Curiously, in a city with a plethora of plaques, the gateway remains anonymous, at least at time of writing. The little nickum, George Gordon, later the poet, Lord Byron, passed through it many times when accompanying his mama to St Paul's Chapel. Johnston and Boswell also passed through it *en route* to worship, facts perhaps worth a mention. Still on the west side about halfway down the Gallowgate, a little group of buildings has somehow escaped demolition. It comprises Ogston

The fine pend archway in its original setting.

& Tennant's former office, the handsome building of the Blue Lamp (the Lumpie) next door, and the sympathetically restored Candle Close Gallery which sells furniture crafts and jewellery. Here one has a glimmer of what

From left to right, Ogston's & Tennant's former office, the Blue Lamp and Candle Close Gallery. Courtesy, Mrs Joan MacMillan.

St Margaret's Episcopal Church, Gallowgate. Courtesy, Mrs Joan MacMillan

might have been.

Back on the east side, things are looking up. The southern foothills of the Porthill are dominated by the Gallowgate's gem, St Margaret's Episcopal Church built on the Ferguson Court site to designs by James Matthews,

The former St Margaret's School, Gallowgate. Courtesy, Mrs Joan MacMillan.

in 1870; the distinctive stonework and red pantiles of its later chapel, added by Sir Ninian Comper in 1890, are a delight. It is still kept company, in its forecourt, by St Margaret's Episcopal School which has the enduring look of the biblical house built on a rock. This, the only surviving Gallowgate school building, is now a branch of Voluntary Services where furniture and bric-a-brac are sold. The interior is 'much altered' but the handsome wooden banister and wrought iron balusters remain.

Leaving the Porthill and moving towards Broad Street, that once hideous pile, Greyfriars House, has had some plastic surgery and now masquerades as a simple neo-Classical temple. This face lift had done its environment a world of good. Finally we reach again the residential block on the former Middle School site, which conveys a sense of appropriateness for the area. When the concrete jumble at the Mounthooly end is eventually pensioned off and a cohesive policy evolved for the Gallowgate as a whole, planners could do worse than look closely at developments at the Broad Street end.

The flats at the Broad Street end of the Gallowgate. They stand on the former site of the Middle School. Courtesy, Mrs Joan MacMillan.

Chapter 14

Full Circle

No area of Aberdeen has been subject to such overwhelming change over the
past three decades as that which includes Causewayend.
Cuthbert Graham, Press & Journal, February 19, 1972

During the early 1970s, the hope was expressed that once the roundabout was completed, Mounthooly would again be one of the great focal
points of the city, as the Gallowgate-head had been in the past. In January
1977 it was open for business, and rather larger than expected. In a typical
Aberdeen way of coming to terms with the untoward, its great size became
the butt of local humour. (The roundabout is officially not a roundabout at
all but a one-way traffic system, a term, one suspects, that is only used by
officials). Walking around it, trying remember where buildings once were
and streets began, is a lengthy and frightening experience. Traffic roars past
and numerous crossings have to be negotiated. It bewilders those who
knew the old lie of the land, for so much has vanished without trace.

Curiously, if one braves the underpasses - they do not have a good
reputation - and climbs on to the top of the roundabout, it becomes the eye
of the storm. In spite of heavy goods vehicles pounding past, there is a
feeling of calm and remoteness. This two and a half acre area of grass and
trees must be the least used of all Aberdeen's parklands, and surely it could
play a more significant role in civic life than it has done. It is an excellent
vantage point to evaluate the changes that took place during the 1960s and

O.K., Mr. Kay, fit can I dae for ye? The Zoo hisna lost een o' its priceless puddocks, his it? Fit? You want me to throw my support behind the Zoo? There's nae need to be personal. Oh, I see fit ye mean. Certainly I will be prepared to attend a public meeting an' spik up for the Zoo. Efter a' the Zoo is one of our finest tourist attractions second only tae the Mounthooly Roundabout an' the Aiberdeen smell.

From the Councillor Swick cartoon published in Leopard Magazine, March 1977.

1970s and assess their impact. We can work clockwise again, starting with West North Street which, in spite of its constant flow of traffic, has a barren look about it, the result of its lack of houses and great width. This is to some extent relieved by the proud silhouette of the Mitchell Hall on the site of the

'...the least used of all Aberdeen's parklands'. The view from the top of the Mounthooly roundabout, north to the newsagent's and the Canal Place flats.

190

The wide sweep of West North Street showing right, the Mitchell Hall and left, Victoria House.

old Marischal College Garden. On the opposite side of the carriageway, the handsome North Lodge looks in good shape. It was once the Victoria Model Lodging House and now as Victoria House, is a hostel for the single homeless.

The engineers are long gone. The Safeway supermarket plies its trade at the very place where the engineers of John M Henderson once wrought. In 1985 this world famous firm sold its four acre site and transferred operations to the Kirkton Industrial Estate in Arbroath, making redundancies in its Aberdeen workforce but employing men from Keith Blackman Engineering, whose premises were taken over. Next door, Barry, Henry & Cook was acquired by the newly established oil service firm, Seaforth Maritime, in 1973 to provide an instant engineering division. Barry, Cook continued to operate under its own name for a few years before eventually vanishing under the Seaforth standard. Victor Cook, chairman of the company and the last of the Cooks was in his seventies at the time of the takeover. He died in 1990 at the age 92, leaving £3.5 million to fund an educational trust in memory of Gordon Cook. But the name of Barry, Henry & (sometimes) Cook lives on in Aberdeen, though at one's feet, inscribed on cast iron manholes and pavement drain covers. Future archaeologists can date them roughly on either side of the 1920s divide, BC and CA according to whether they are Before Cook or Cook Added.

191

Mulco, as noted, had moved to custom-built premises in St Machar Road in 1954, where the firm continued to expand its considerable range of engineering services, adding maritime and industrial divisions, and successfully taking up the challenges offered by North Sea Oil. The old premises at No 184 West North Street were demolished to make way for the dual carriageway. Much of West North Street from the former Barry, Henry site, north to the back of the 'Globie' is now devoted to the service of the motor car.

Moving across to the Gallowgate, to Porthill and Seamount Courts and their neighbours, attempts have been made to minimise the ugliness of this pocket council estate with a scattering of flower pots, iron-girt young trees and an array of 'antique' bollards. Worthwhile though such efforts are, these structures, and the fortress-like Technical College, now the Gallowgate Centre of the Aberdeen College, remain stubbornly uninviting and inaccessible, at least so it seems to the passer-by. This is one of the city's most historic areas, the site of the port, the gallows and the windmill and it deserves better.

If the Porthill is an eyesore, Spring Garden today is an example of modern building in sympathy with the environment. In 1992, after two hundred years on the same site, McKinnon's moved out. The firm had

The flats of Loch Court, left, on the old Milne Cruden site, with the students' flats of Spring Garden opposite. This was the corner where the lade turned to flow along the Lochside.

latterly occupied only about 35 per cent of the space there, and more conveniently-sized premises in Pittodrie Street had become available. Prior to demolition, a careful record was made of the Spring Garden Iron Works, one of Aberdeen's most interesting examples of industrial architecture. Details of pend, gable and iron work of the student accommodation now built on the site strongly hint of the old Iron Works. That is not surprising. No less that 3000 blocks of good quality granite were set aside from the down-takings, and have been re-used in the ground floor and for the voussoirs - the wedge-shaped stones of the arches - near the Gallowgate end. And so, like Barry, Henry, the Spring Garden Iron Works lives on in its own individual way. The student accommodation has been thoughtfully designed by Angus Taylor, the scale well-suited to the existing townscape. Meanwhile, in Pittodrie Street, W. McKinnon & Co, with a staff of a dozen, continue to manufacture and to sell coffee plantation equipment to the coffee growing countries of world. They are no longer ironfounders. Castings, more economically, are bought in from a Larbert foundry, but the firm's export record of ninety-eight percent of its output is as brilliant as ever.

Back in Spring Garden, the sturdy Spring Gardens Works of Milne, Cruden & Co, though derelict, survived until the 1980s as did the premises of William Paterson & Sons Ltd. While the latter building lay unused, police dogs and their handlers found its rambling layout ideal to practice sniffing out suspicious characters. After demolition, the flats of Loch Court were built on the site by the City of Aberdeen and blend neatly with the townscape. At the George Street end, William Paterson's residence of Spring Garden House has also gone. In 1938 the warehouse that was built over the garden became Donald's Ice Rink. The House itself was boarded up, though its basement remained in use as a changing area for the rink. House and rink have gone now, replaced by modern flats and only the original wall of Spring Garden House remains. Much of Spring Garden - sometimes reverting to its plural form these days - is now a modest and acceptable mix of restored and new buildings.
Continuing clockwise, Gerrard Street, blocked off now at the Mounthooly end, has been attractively redeveloped. The old tenements at the east end have gone, and the street's great feature is the handsome Gerrard Street Baptist Church whose wood-panelled entrance looks welcoming when the doors are open. Nearby is the Dee Swimming and Humane Club, an early building at 'new' Mounthooly. It would be acceptable on a playing field perhaps, but its proximity to the grandeur of the church accentuates its hut-like features. Nevertheless, zebra stripes of grey and brown provide a satisfactory camouflage. Beside it, a children's

A childrens' playground near Gerrard Street, with the Dee Swimming Club beyond.

playground adds a touch of colour. At the George Street end of Gerrard Street there is a blend of the old and the new, a block of renovated tenements on the south side, which narrowly escaped demolition, and opposite, a block of flats in cream and brown, whose adventurous fenestration reflects the windows and chimneys of the tenements opposite. The scheme was carried out by the City of Aberdeen, with Ian Ross as architect in charge of the rehabilitation, while Mike Pastard worked on the new flats. The project, which showed what can be done with a bit of imagination, received an Aberdeen Civic Society Commendation in 1982.

Catherine Street has become as anonymous as the original lady. From the Mounthooly end, however, one can look across to the gigantic Broadford lums, and there is a glimpse of one of the stately houses of George Street, long converted into flats and hidden behind a row of tenements. Viewed from the George Street end, Catherine Street is a rump of little more than cassies and landscaping, blocked off by Hutcheon Court, which with its fellow high rise, Greig Court, named after a former city housing convener, is another unlovely legacy of the mid-sixties. John Knox's kirk, rendered dwarf-like by the multi-storeys, can be glimpsed in the distance.

As we approach Hutcheon Street the curvilinear gables of the former Comb Works can be sighted, and the old building is as high and handsome as ever. Another oil-related firm, AMEC Offshore Developments Ltd, experts in offshore engineering, has been resident there since the late 1980s,

Gerrard Street in 1995 looking east towards Mounthooly. The buildings beyond the traditional tenements, right, form part of the Spring Garden student accommodation. Modern flats, left, have replaced the condemned tenements which are glimpsed beyond the church in the picture on page 164.

All that remains of Catherine Street. Looking from Mounthooly towards George Street, with the Broadford lums standing guard.

and where once there was horn and hoof, there are now drawing boards and engineering equipment. Hutcheon Street itself has been improved by opening out, and by landscaping.

Round now to Causewayend, where in 1995, something new, a neat, spruce, chapel-like building appeared opposite the school. It is not a another church, however, but the premises of Aberdeen Funeral Services, no great distance but very different from Ben Cormack's old parlour. It sits amidst the motor accessories, car services, and tyre companies that now

Something new in Causewayend - the spruce parlour of Aberdeen Funeral Services. A part of the former Hutcheon Street Comb Works is seen to the left.

proliferate in Causewayend. Further along, in Powis Place the tenements beside old Cassie-end Kirk have survived, but opposite there has been demolition and a row of modern flats has appeared. Nearby, the Froghall Community Centre, another example of the 'camouflage' school of architecture, hides modestly behind some bushes. Canal Road, as we know, has become a cul-de-sac. R G Garvie & Sons, hoping once to expand there, vanished altogether, taken over by United States Steel. The Canal Place cul-de-sac was cleared of its assorted Nissen huts, warehouses and once genteel houses, and is now filled with modern housing. Munro's Transport, the local haulage firm which started off at Mounthooly, has, like Mulco, long since departed to St Machar Road where as the Munro Transport Group, it operates haulage, distribution and storage divisions, and has several branches in Scotland, as well as in Manchester and London.

Between Canal Road and Canal Street, and beyond, the tracks of the old GNSR Waterloo Line still lie on the former canal bed. The line remains in use. A 'ghost train' or to be less romantic, a goods train of rail tanks, filled with chemicals, makes the journey towards Waterloo Quay once or twice a week. South of the Miller Street Tarry Briggie, however, the consignment goes direct to the Croxton & Gary depot beside the old Waterloo goods yard on a single line. Those lines which terminated within the Waterloo yard, were lifted in the early 1990s. As traffic pounds round Mounthooly, one can't help feeling that much more use might have been made of the Waterloo Line which offered direct access to the docks, and very easily still could.

Traffic dominates Mounthooly, yet the philosophy which brought about the creation of the roundabout and sacrificed a community to the Juggernaut is now outmoded. One current opinion is that the car and the lorry, these noisy, smelly pollutants, just like the factory lums of yore, have no place in the city centre. Far too much valuable space is given over to them. What is required, this argument continues, is that people should be able to live near their workplace, and all should be focused around the city centre. Former residents of Mounthooly and Causewayend must see the irony here.

Continuing to spy out the land from the roundabout, Causewayend School and John Knox's Church remain the majestic guardians of Mounthooly. But apart from students walking to and fro from King's College, intent on negotiating the roundabout, these streets, or what is left of them, once so full of life, are now sparsely populated. After the diaspora brought about by the joint forces of redevelopment and road improvement, residents were rehoused elsewhere, in Mastrick or Kincorth, for example,

'Causewayend School and John Knox's Church remain the guardians of Mounthooly'.

197

and were settled in there, long before new or refurbished accommodation around Mounthooly became available. As far as one can judge, a few locals took the opportunity to return to the area when new housing was offered, but not as many, it seems, as returned to Woodside when a similar situation prevailed there.

Those who have remained near their old haunts pop into the Mounthooly Newsagent for a news. It is a focal point, the lone survivor of an area that once teemed with shops. Though now run by Alan Anderson, many older folk continue to call it 'Mackie's' from the days when it was run by John and Grace McIntosh. Their daughter, Mrs Dempster, keeps the old link, popping in for her Sunday papers, as do others when they skail from John Knox's. Much affection and nostalgia for the old community remains. Alex Slessor can still recall the individual

Newsagent Alan Anderson holds the fort in Mounthooly.

and distinctive smells of the Comb Works, Soapy Ogston's, Broadford and the Jute Factory in Froghall. But these are perhaps best evoked in the memory.

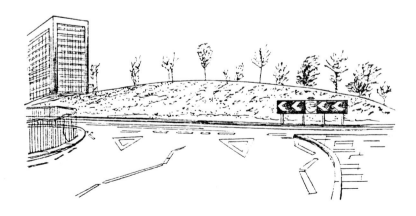

198

Select Bibliography

Books consulted
Anderson, Robert, *Aberdeen in Bygone Days*, Aberdeen Daily Journal, 1910
Buchan, Peter, *Autobiographical Sketch*, Glasgow 1839
Burnett, John George, (ed) *Powis Papers, 1507-1894*, Third Spalding Club, 1951
Fraser, G M, *The Lone Sheiling*, The Bon-Accord Press, 1908
Fraser, G M, and Henderson, Moira, *Aberdeen Street Names*, James G Bisset, 1986
Gammie, Alexander, *The Churches of Aberdeen*, Aberdeen Daily Journal, 1909
Keith, Alexander, *A Thousand Years of Aberdeen*, Aberdeen University Press, 1972
Kennedy William, *The Annals of Aberdeen*, London 1818
Mackinnon, Lachlan, *Recollections of an Old Lawyer*, D Wyllie & Son, 1935
Meldrum, Edward, *Aberdeen of Old*, 1986
Reid, John S, *Mechanical Aberdeen*, KMP / JSR 1990
Thomson, Michael, *Silver Screen in the Silver City*, Aberdeen University Press, 1988

Booklets
Diack, William, *The Rise and Progress of the Granite Industry in Aberdeen*, Reprint from Quarry Manager's Journal, 1949
Duncan, Robert, *Textiles and Toil*, Aberdeen City Libraries, 1984,
Patrick, John, *The Coming of Turnpikes to Aberdeenshire*, Centre for Scottish Studies, Aberdeen Univeristy, 1981
Youngson, Flora, *Dominie's Daughter*, Centre for Scottish Studies, Aberdeen University, 1991

Bazaar Books
Book of Powis, James A Coutts (ed), 1906; *Causewayend Free Church*,1900; *Gallowgate United Free*, 1904; *John Knox Parish Church, Aberdeen*, 1910.

Works of Reference
Aberdeen Post Office Directories
Aberdeen Pub Companion, Archibald Hopkin, 1975
Aberdeen Today, Henry Munro, Aberdeen, 1907
City of Aberdeen, The Statistical Account of Aberdeenshire, William Blackwood, 1843
Granite City: A Plan for Aberdeen, W Dobson Chapman & C F Riley, Batsford 1952
In Memoriam, Wm Kay & Sons, Aberdeen, annually 1890-1910
Municipal Affairs in Aberdeen, 1833-1888, D Wyllie & Son, Aberdeen 1889
Scotland of Today Part II, Historical Publishing Coy, 1889

Periodicals
Aberdeen Chamber of Commerce Journal
Industry in the North East of Scotland: No 2 *Mechanical Handling*, October, 1955: No 45 *Machinery for Export*, December, 1966: No 66 *Engineering Specialists*, March 1972. (All anon)

Aberdeen University Review
John S Reid, 'Patrick Copland 1748-1822', Autumn, 1984
Leopard Magazine
Gibb, Bob, 'Memories Raised of Gallowgate Days', March 1995
Grant, Deirdre, 'John Williams of Tyseal', March, 1982
MacDonald, Ian R, 'The Gaelic Congregation', October, 1985
Morgan, Diane, 'The Life and Times of Tommy Scott Sutherland', Part 5, May, 1976
Watson, Iain, 'Harry Gordon, Part 1', November, 1977

Monographs
Anderson, A F, 'Some Early Experiments in Applied Electromagnetism', March 10, 1975
Gordon, George, 'A Short History of King's Crescent', Aberdeen, 1985
Souter, John, A, 'Gallowgate Area', Aberdeen, January 14, 1988

Newspaper Articles
Graham, Cuthbert, 'Quick Change Causewayend', Press & Journal February 19, 1972
Jenkins, G Gordon, 'Old Roads out of Aberdeen', Aberdeen Free Press, June 11, 1919

Primary Source Material
Aberdeen City Archives: miscellaneous deeds relating to the Gallowgate-head: Commutation Books, 1811-1812, 1824-25, 1839-1840.
Aberdeen City Libraries: Various Aberdeen Touncil Council Minutes from 1893; Census Returns, 1851, 1871, 1891: cuttings from the *Aberdeen Journal*, the *Press & Journal*, the *Evening Express:*
Grampian Regional Archives: Miscellaneous Valuation Rolls from 1855. School Log Books of Causewayend and Middle Schools .

Index

The Villages of Aberdeen
Footdee

Diane Morgan

ISBN 1 898645 01 9

What the Press said about 'Footdee'

Footdee book tops sales list.
Aberdeen Press and Journal

A model of what a local history should be.
Scottish Book Collector

Aa tellt by a flowin pen.
Robbie Shepherd: Press and Journal

She writes with warmth and affection.
Bob Smith: Leopard Magazine

A comprehensive insight into a fascinating village.
Aberdeen University Review

This book is rich in fact. There is a lot here for £10.95.
Scottish Local History Forum

A painstakingly researched history of Aberdeen's famous fishing village and the shipyards of the Duthies, Walter Hood, Alexander Hall and Hall Russell.
Scots Magazine

'The 1993 best sellers in Aberdeen were *Bravo Two Zero*, Baroness Thatcher's *The Downing Street Years*, Jung Chang's *Wild Swans*, and *The Villages of Aberdeen - Footdee* by Diane Morgan.' Dillons Bookshop quoted in the *Evening Express*.